# IMMIGRATION ISSUES
## IN AMERICA

## By Michelle Denton

Portions of this book originally appeared in *Immigration* by Richard Brownell.

Published in 2018 by
**Lucent Press, an Imprint of Greenhaven Publishing, LLC**
353 3rd Avenue
Suite 255
New York, NY 10010

Designer: Seth Hughes
Editor: Jennifer Lombardo

**Cataloging-in-Publication Data**

Names: Denton, Michelle.
Title: Immigration issues in America / Michelle Denton.
Description: New York : Lucent Press, 2018. | Series: Hot topics | Includes index.
Identifiers: ISBN 9781534561519 (library bound) | ISBN 9781534561526 (ebook)
Subjects: LCSH: Emigration and immigration law–United States–Juvenile literature. | United States–Emigration and immigration–Juvenile literature.
Classification: LCC KF4819.85 D46 2018 | DDC 343.7308'2–dc23

Printed in the United States of America

CPSIA compliance information: Batch #BS17KL: For further information contact Greenhaven Publishing LLC, New York, New York at 1-844-317-7404.

Please visit our website, www.greenhavenpublishing.com. For a free color catalog of all our high-quality books, call toll free 1-844-317-7404 or fax 1-844-317-7405.

# CONTENTS

Adolescence is a time when many people begin to take notice of the world around them. News channels, blogs, and talk radio shows are constantly promoting one view or another; very few are unbiased. Young people also hear conflicting information from parents, friends, teachers, and acquaintances. Often, they will hear only one side of an issue or be given flawed information. People who are trying to support a particular viewpoint may cite inaccurate facts and statistics on their blogs, and news programs present many conflicting views of important issues in our society. In a world where it seems everyone has a platform to share their thoughts, it can be difficult to find unbiased, accurate information about important issues.

It is not only facts that are important. In blog posts, in comments on online videos, and on talk shows, people will share opinions that are not necessarily true or false, but can still have a strong impact. For example, many young people struggle with their body image. Seeing or hearing negative comments about particular body types online can have a huge effect on the way someone views himself or herself and may lead to depression and anxiety. Although it is important not to keep information hidden from young people under the guise of protecting them, it is equally important to offer encouragement on issues that affect their mental health.

The titles in the Hot Topics series provide readers with different viewpoints on important issues in today's society. Many of these issues, such as teen pregnancy and Internet safety, are of immediate concern to young people. This series aims to give readers factual context on these crucial topics in a way that lets them form their own opinions. The facts presented throughout also serve to empower readers to help themselves or support people they know who are struggling with many of the challenges adolescents face today. Although negative viewpoints are not ignored or downplayed, this series allows young people to see that the challenges they face are not insurmountable. Eating disorders can be overcome, the Internet can be navigated safely, and pregnant teens do not have to feel hopeless.

Quotes encompassing all viewpoints are presented and cited so readers can trace them back to their original source, verifying for themselves whether the information comes from a reputable place. Additional books and websites are listed, giving readers a starting point from which to continue their own research. Chapter questions encourage discussion, allowing young people to hear and understand their classmates' points of view as they further solidify their own. Full-color photographs and enlightening charts provide a deeper understanding of the topics at hand. All of these features augment the informative text, helping young people understand the world they live in and formulate their own opinions concerning the best way they can improve it.

# The Great Immigration Debate

Immigration has always been a controversial subject in the United States. Aside from Native Americans, every person living in the country either has ancestors who immigrated from other countries or is a recent immigrant themselves. Despite this, many Americans throughout history have insisted on drawing lines between "real" Americans and immigrants, who they view as foreigners. Millions of immigrants have come to this country throughout American history, hoping to find a better life than the one they left behind, but many are forced to continue to fight for the rights given to those who came before them.

The 2016 presidential election became an arena for the debate surrounding immigration, particularly in the case of people coming from Mexico. Currently, among the 20 million Hispanic immigrants in the United States, approximately 7.8 million are here illegally, meaning they crossed the border unauthorized or chose to stay after their temporary visas expired. Because of the number of unauthorized immigrants, the United States must change the way it thinks about and deals with immigration. The resulting debate over how to handle immigration has become one of the most divisive topics in recent history. Immigration impacts how the nation conducts business, how it governs the population, and how Americans see themselves as individuals and as a society. However, there are differing opinions as to how the country should move forward with immigrants in mind.

## The March Continues

In 2007, immigrants and their supporters gathered across the country to protest proposals in Congress that would crack down on illegal immigration. Many of the marchers were workers in service industry jobs who had lived in the United States for years but who feared deportation because they were unauthorized immigrants. "After working 22 years here, paying taxes, and being a good citizen, I think it's fair they give me residency," said Los Angeles, California, protester Manuel Hernandez, an unauthorized immigrant from Mexico who marched with his wife and two children. "It's not fair we don't have documents."[1]

*Immigrants want to be treated as human beings, not as a problem.*

Hernandez's story was one that was repeated by many of the 20,000 protestors in Los Angeles that day. In Chicago, Illinois, 150,000 took to the streets to protest the breakup of mixed-status families, or families made up of authorized and unauthorized immigrants who could be split up if federal authorities arrested and deported mothers or fathers who could not prove their documented residency status. A gathering of 5,000 in New York City called for an end to immigration raids that rounded up thousands of unauthorized immigrants.

The nationwide event occurred peacefully, with the exception of a scuffle between police in Los Angeles and a small group of protestors who threw bottles and rocks. Organizers and participants wanted to demonstrate that undocumented workers are hard-working, law-abiding people worthy of citizenship, but several counter-demonstrators voiced opposition to granting citizenship to millions of unauthorized immigrants.

Jerry Hearty of Coolidge, Arizona, was one counter-demonstrator who lost his union-wage job in a meatpacking plant in Nebraska many years before when the company started hiring immigrants at lower wages. He claimed, "Now, no American can work at a packinghouse anymore because it's all minimum wage, and it's all illegal aliens."[2] People like Hearty do not blame the companies seeking cheap labor but instead blame immigrants, whom they believe should follow the legal process of becoming citizens.

Today, the concerns of both sides are almost the same. In the weeks following the 2016 presidential election and the weeks following the inauguration of President Donald Trump, peaceful protests sprang up across the country in support of marginalized groups, including immigrants. One of their main concerns was the new administration's threat of deportation toward millions of unauthorized but hard-working people. Mass deportation, in many people's opinion, is not the answer to America's problems. Not only would mixed-status families be ripped apart, but the government expense and sudden lack of workers would not help the economy the way some claim. Many hope the future holds a pathway to U.S. citizenship for unauthorized immigrants, rather than a road back to the countries they left to seek a better life.

*Some believe unauthorized immigrants, whom they call illegal aliens, are getting rights they feel should be reserved for U.S. citizens and authorized noncitizens.*

## Remaining a Land of Opportunity

The protests of May 2007, as well as their much larger predecessors that occurred from March through May 2006, gave voice to many views about immigration in the United States and to theories about what should be done with the undocumented population. The 2006 events were triggered by debate over a major immigration reform bill that was being considered by federal lawmakers in Washington, D.C. Not only would an unauthorized immigrant be immediately arrested, fined, and deported, but the immigrant in question and anyone who helped them remain in the United States would be classified as a felon.

Protestors wanted to have their opinions heard by elected officials, and they refused to be sidelined while their future was decided. Unfortunately, the protests did not have the effect unauthorized immigrants and their citizen supporters desired. A protest on May 1, 2006, with 1 million demonstrators nationwide, led to a backlash against illegal immigration. In the year following that event, several states passed strict laws against hiring unauthorized immigrants and prohibited them from accessing government services such as health care and social welfare. A federal push for stricter enforcement led to the deportation of about 281,000 unauthorized immigrants in 2006, up 35,000 from the previous year. In 2007, more than 319,000 were deported, indicating that the trend was increasing substantially. This backlash was a major reason for the large drop-off in participation in the 2007 demonstrations. Many undocumented immigrants feared being identified among the marchers and chose to stay away, rather than risk being arrested.

The number of deportations decreased steadily during the last years of the Obama administration; in 2015, about 81,000 fewer people were deported than were deported in 2014. Despite this trend, unauthorized immigrants still live in fear. Because of the absence of constructive solutions to the immigration problems in America, those who believe undocumented immigrants are the cause of both economic and social destruction are calling for strict reforms that may ultimately do more harm than good. Although some would disagree, immigrants have shaped America since before it became a country.

At stake is the future of immigration in the United States. America is often seen as a land of opportunity by people in other countries looking to improve their lives. If it is to maintain this image, it will need to reconcile the conflict that exists between some people's fantasies of a "perfect" America and the reality of being a first-world country in the 21st century.

# CHAPTER 1

# A Nation of Immigrants

The European settlers who colonized North America came to the New World seeking wealth and freedom, much like the immigrants who come to the United States every year. However, they do not fit today's definition of "immigrant"—"a person who comes to a country to take up permanent residence"[3]—since there was technically no country to take up residence in, and the colonists' presence in Native American territory was far more disruptive to life on this continent than that of modern immigrants. Unlike today's immigrants, colonists from Spain, France, England, and the Netherlands conquered the native people who lived there before them and began erasing their culture, replacing it with a recreation of European society—one that predominately benefited white, Christian people. Since then, each new group of immigrants has left its mark on American culture, but none have so fundamentally changed it.

As it declared itself an independent nation in 1776, the United States also established itself as a beacon of hope for the huddled masses around the world. As a country founded on the principle that all people are created equal and with the right to "Life, Liberty, and the pursuit of Happiness," as the Declaration of Independence says, it was primed from the beginning to become a destination for those who wanted a better life. Governed by a democratically elected legislature, America was truly a novelty in the 18th and 19th centuries, and it attracted those who were being oppressed by monarchies and dictatorships in their home countries. It also operated on a free market economy that allowed virtually anyone to go into business for themselves, and it seemed that the only limit to a person's success in America was how hard they were willing to work. Immigrants came to the United States expecting to be welcomed with open arms. The romantic notion was that their ethnicity, religion, and social status would be of little consequence after they became full citizens—Americans before anything else. Becoming a citizen, however, was no easy task.

To immigrate to the United States, people voyaged across thousands of miles of ocean from Europe and Asia, or crossed the barren desert region separating the United States from Central and South America. Leaving families that they often never saw again, immigrants sometimes came to this country with little or no knowledge of the English language or American customs. Although many new jobs were created as the Industrial Revolution came to America and the country spread westward, there was never enough work for everyone, and immigrants were often taken advantage of by employers and landlords. Living conditions in the cities where most immigrants settled were crowded and unsanitary, which led to disease as well as cultural conflict as people from vastly differing countries were forced to live in close proximity to each other. Outside their communities, they were faced with bigotry and hatred from native-born Americans who saw them as lesser.

Despite these hardships, immigrants continued to arrive in the United States in large numbers. The opportunity to make life better for themselves and their families was too good for people to be deterred by the stories they may have heard about the mistreatment of their fellow immigrants. To many, anything was possible in America, and the struggle was more than worth it.

## THE AMERICAN DREAM

"… that dream of a land in which life should be better and richer and fuller for everyone, with opportunity for each according to ability or achievement. It is a difficult dream for the European upper classes to interpret adequately, and too many of us ourselves have grown weary and mistrustful of it. It is not a dream of motor cars and high wages merely, but a dream of social order in which each man and each woman shall be able to attain to the fullest stature of which they are innately capable, and be recognized by others for what they are, regardless of the fortuitous circumstances of birth or position."
–James Truslow Adams, author

James Truslow Adams, *The Epic of America*. Boston, MA: Little, Brown, and Co., 1931, pp. 214-215.

## From Western Europe

The small amount of immigration to the United States in the early years of the American republic was not well documented, and the best population estimates combined with passenger manifests of ships arriving in American ports place the yearly average at 6,000 people up until 1820. The U.S. Census—a survey taken every 10 years to determine how many people live in the United States—was first conducted in 1790, but it only counted the number of free men and women, as well as the number of enslaved Africans. It did not inquire about a person's nation of origin, and it was quite simplistic compared to the modern census, which includes questions about what kind of housing a person lives in, where they are from, whether they have a disability, their income, and more.

Turmoil in Europe as a result of the French Revolution of 1789 and the Napoleonic Wars that devastated Europe until 1814 significantly limited immigration. Many able-bodied men were drafted into armies of the various warring nations, and Europe's war-ravaged economy left little money for private citizens to buy passage on a ship. A number of private shipping companies were pressed into military service or went out of business, so there was considerably less transatlantic travel. The War of 1812 between the United States and Great Britain also curtailed immigration because there is little motivation to immigrate to a nation that is at war.

After this period of upheaval, a sustained period of prosperity in the United States led to enormous economic and territorial expansion—two factors that proved very inviting to would-be immigrants. Over 2.5 million immigrants came to America in a 30-year period beginning in 1820, playing an important role in the rapid growth of the population, which rose from 9.6 million that year to just over 23 million in 1850, which was one of the highest growth rates in the world at that time.

A vast majority of these immigrants came from Western Europe, with the bulk of them from Germany, Ireland, France, and Great Britain. The Irish were driven to America by widespread famine, while the rest of the European arrivals were mainly motivated by economic factors. Europe was rapidly industrializing during this time, and a large number of agricultural jobs disappeared as land and labor were lost to factories and commercial expansion. While the United States was also industrializing at an accelerated rate, there was far more land available for agricultural development. Additionally, the development of steamships and railroads further facilitated the ease of travel across Europe to the coast, where passage could be obtained to cross the Atlantic Ocean to America.

*This is a replica of the* Jeanie Johnston, *a "famine ship" that carried 2,000 immigrants from Ireland between 1848 and 1855.*

According to Herbert S. Klein, author of *A Population History of the United States*, "The post-1830 transoceanic immigration to the United States would turn out to be the largest such oceanic migration in world history."[4]

## "No Irish Need Apply"

Although it may be an urban myth that this sentiment appeared on virtually every "Help Wanted" sign during a period of time in the 1800s, some 19th-century newspaper ads for female domestics did indeed include the words, "No Irish need apply." Richard Jensen of the University of Chicago argued, "Evidence from the job market shows no significant discrimination against the Irish—on the contrary, employers eagerly sought them out."[1]

However, the reason for their popularity may have been their willingness to work for low wages at hazardous tasks. According to the Library of Congress:

*Irish immigrants often entered the workforce at the bottom of the occupational ladder and took on the menial and dangerous jobs that were often avoided by other workers. Many Irish women became servants or domestic workers, while many Irish men labored in coal mines and built railroads and canals. Railroad construction was so dangerous that it was said, "[there was] an Irishman buried under every tie."*

*As Irish immigrants moved inland from eastern cities, they found themselves in heated competition for jobs ... This competition heightened class tensions and, at the turn of the century, Irish Americans were often antagonized by organizations such as the American Protective Association (APA) and the Ku Klux Klan.*[2]

1. Richard Jensen, "'No Irish Need Apply': A Myth of Victimization," *Journal of Social History* 36, no. 2 (2002): 405-429. tigger.uic.edu/~rjensen/no-irish.htm.
2. "Irish—Joining the Workforce," Library of Congress. www.loc.gov/teachers/classroommaterials/presentationsandactivities/presentations/immigration/alt/irish4.html.

Beginning in 1850, the American population began to feel the effects of large-scale immigration. Until 1830, immigrants accounted for only 1.5 percent of the population. By 1850, when the U.S. Census began recording place of birth, immigrants had risen to nearly 10 percent of the population. The California Gold Rush of 1849 brought the first significant wave of immigration from nations outside Europe, with immigrants arriving from China, Australia, Mexico, and South America. Additionally, the end of the Mexican War in 1848 resulted in the United States gaining a large amount of territory from Mexico, leading to the automatic U.S. citizenship of about 75,000 Mexicans living in that region.

Europeans continued to dominate immigration during this period, despite the addition of these other nationalities. Between 1850 and 1930, 5 million Germans immigrated to the United States, along with 3.5 million British and 4.5 million Irish. The onset of the American Civil War in 1861 slowed immigration, and the foreign-born population of the United States grew by only a little more than 1 million during this period, but after 1880, it picked up again.

# Composition of Immigration
United States, 1840–1860

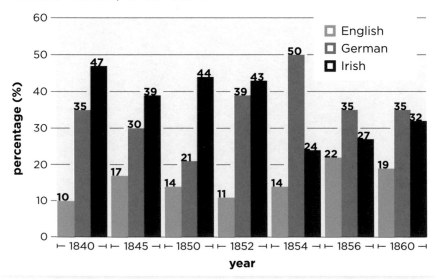

*Irish and German people made up the majority of immigrants to the United States in the mid-1840s, as this information from the U.S. Census Bureau shows.*

# From Southern and Eastern Europe

While immigrants continued to arrive in a steady stream from Western Europe, the number who arrived from Southern and Eastern Europe began to rise sharply in the last decades of the 19th century. The industrialization and resultant economic prosperity in Western Europe did not spread to the south and east, and immigrants from those areas fled the poor economic and social conditions with growing frequency. In 1870, the Census reported 93,824 foreign-born persons from Eastern and Southern Europe, which accounted for 6 percent of all immigrants. By 1910, over 4.5 million foreign-born persons from Eastern and Southern Europe were living in the United States, coming mainly from Poland, Russia, and Italy. By this point, nearly two-thirds of all immigrants came from Eastern and Southern Europe.

With the arrival of people from this region, the general makeup of European immigration began to change, and with it, America's attitude toward immigrants. Most of the immigrants from Western Europe were light-skinned and generally of the Protestant religion, which was the predominant religious faith of the United States. The Irish, many of whom were Catholic, were a notable exception, and they faced numerous difficulties in the United States because of their faith. Groups of Protestant Americans, such as the Order of the Star-Spangled Banner and the Order of United Americans, heaped scorn and ridicule—and sometimes violence—upon Catholics from Ireland and other nations, mainly because they feared that the continued arrival of Catholic immigrants would threaten the Protestant majority in the United States. Irish Catholics in particular were sometimes turned away by employers and ended up taking public-sector jobs in many cities as police officers and other municipal workers.

Many of the immigrants from Eastern and Southern Europe also faced racism because they had darker skin, which made them visibly different from the majority of the population. Jewish immigrants often remained within their own communities and rarely mixed with outsiders, which made many native-born Americans suspicious of them. Their religion was looked upon as strange by many citizens in a nation that was overwhelmingly Christian.

Jews, Irish, and other immigrants from Europe often settled in urban areas that were predominantly poor and filthy. The conditions of these neighborhoods were a result of poor urban planning and a complete lack of municipal services, such as trash collection, sewage treatment, and health codes—all things

*Many immigrants found themselves in small, cramped housing, such as these New York tenements.*

taken for granted today. However, the immigrants were blamed for the squalid conditions of the inner cities.

In fact, immigrants were more often than not blamed for society's ills. Francis Walker captured how many native-born Americans felt toward European immigrants in the *Atlantic Monthly* in 1896:

> *For nearly two generations, great numbers of persons utterly unable to earn their living, by reason of one or another form of physical or mental disability, and others who were, from widely different causes, unfit to be members of any decent community, were admitted to our ports without challenge or question.*
>
> *The question to-day is, not of preventing the wards of our almshouses, our insane asylums, and our jails from being stuffed to repletion by new arrivals from Europe; but of protecting the American rate of wages, the American standard of living, and the quality of American citizenship from degradation through the tumultuous access of vast throngs of ignorant and brutalized peasantry from the countries of eastern and southern Europe.[5]*

Walker implied that immigrants are universally poor, stupid, and violent, and he suggested that America should not expose itself to such people for fear of degrading its culture. Although these beliefs are based in ignorance, they were surprisingly popular then and are still used in arguments against immigration today.

## Turning Off the Tap

Immigration policy was left mainly to the states for the first 70 years of U.S. history, but a series of Supreme Court decisions in 1849—known as the Passenger Cases—began chipping away at state control. The federal government had grown angry at the collection of special taxes from immigrants by several states, and the Supreme Court ruled that they did not have the power to collect such taxes. Congress went further in 1864, passing legislation that took control of immigration policy from the states, and by 1875, the Supreme Court had effectively ruled that the establishment and regulation of immigration policy fell under the federal government's constitutional power to regulate interstate commerce. This was done in part to bring order to a system in which scattered state procedures over immigration often contradicted one another.

Once these Supreme Court precedents were established, the federal government stepped in to create a structured system to control immigration. The first federal act to deliberately set a standard was the Chinese Exclusion Act of 1882. This act rose out of complaints about Chinese immigrants, more than 300,000 of whom had settled in the Western United States since the California Gold Rush, seeking to escape turbulent political conditions in China. Many found work as cheap labor on the railroads and as domestic servants in California and the western territories, where they were blamed for driving down wages. The Exclusion Act's passage barred Chinese immigration to the United States for a period of 10 years and was renewed several times until it was repealed in 1943.

*Immigrants are shown here watching from the deck of their ships as Ellis Island comes into view.*

In 1892, when the 9.2 million immigrants in the United States represented 15 percent of the total population, the federal government took control of immigration at the Port of New York, establishing Ellis Island as the national reception center for people seeking entry into the United States. Everyone who came to Ellis Island and other ports of entry was subjected to literacy tests and health examinations. Those with tuberculosis or other contagious diseases were either turned back or forced to live in quarantine for extended periods of time. The literacy tests were an attempt to control the quality of immigrants who were let into the country. People were further evaluated for the labor skills they possessed, which allowed the government to keep an overabundance of workers with particular job skills from driving down wages for citizens.

In 1907, Senator William P. Dillingham established the U.S. Immigration Commission. This body, historically known as the Dillingham Commission, investigated the occupations and living standards of immigrants in the United States and came to the biased conclusion that immigrants from Eastern and Southern Europe were at a higher risk for criminal behavior, poverty, illness, and lower intelligence than immigrants who had come to America previously.

## THE FREEDOM TO IMMIGRATE

"Liberty depends on a society that allows people the freedom to migrate and live where they can best build a life for themselves. A society that has to compete to attract new and productive citizens will be compelled by necessity to fight for the freedom of its members—even for those who were afforded fewer legal rights because of the circumstances of their birth."
—Brendan Miniter, former assistant editor of the *Wall Street Journal*

Brendan Miniter, "Let Their People Come," *Wall Street Journal*, July 3, 2003

Based in part on the results of the Dillingham Commission, the federal government passed a series of strict immigration quotas to limit the number of people coming from foreign shores. The Emergency Quota Act of 1921 limited the number of immigrants from each nation to 3 percent of that nation's total immigrant population in the United States as reported in the 1910 Census. This act heavily favored immigration from Western Europe because immigrants had been coming from that region for much longer, resulting in higher populations in the United States. The National Origins Act of 1924 further restricted immigration from each country to 2 percent of that nation's total immigrant population in the United States in 1890. Together, these acts greatly reduced mass immigration in the United States for much of the rest of the 20th century.

## Twentieth-Century Immigration

Because of the passage of the two immigration laws, as well as the Great Depression in the 1930s, the number of immigrants steadily decreased. Between 1930 and 1940, the number of immigrants in the country dropped from 14.2 million to 11.5 million.

World War II continued to keep immigration low, but the federal government did allow several thousand Mexican laborers into the country to work in agricultural jobs. Known as the Bracero Program (*bracero* is the Spanish word for "worker"), this use of temporary labor offset the large number of jobs left open by the drafting of millions of male U.S. citizens into the armed forces. Between 1942 and 1964, 4.6 million contracts were signed, although some people came back multiple times on different contracts.

After the Allied victory brought an end to World War II in 1945, the American economy grew tremendously, but immigration was still controlled by strict quotas. The McCarran-Walter Immigration Act of 1952 reaffirmed the national-origins quota system, allowing only 154,277 visas to be issued each year. The act also put an end to the exclusion of Asian immigrants. Various refugee relief acts did allow individuals from war-torn countries in Europe and Asia into the United States in the late 1940s and early 1950s, although many people opposed these acts. Additionally, the War Brides Acts of 1945 and 1946 allowed foreign-born wives and fiancées of U.S. servicemen to immigrate.

In 1954, the federal government carried out a mass deportation of thousands of undocumented immigrants from Mexico. It was estimated in the decade preceding this deportation the number of undocumented immigrants had risen 6,000 percent, with one million coming in 1954 alone, taking advantage of the open border and high number of available jobs. The U.S. Border Patrol, with the help of federal, state, and local authorities in

Texas, Arizona, New Mexico, and California, succeeded in returning many to Mexico. It was unknown exactly how many returned to their native country of their own choice and whether they remained in Mexico or simply crossed back into the United States after the sweep ended.

## The Mid-Century and Beyond

In 1965, the U.S. Congress passed the Hart-Celler Act, which effectively removed many of the immigration quotas that had been in place for decades. An annual limit of 170,000 visas was established for immigrants from countries in the Eastern Hemisphere with no more than 20,000 per country. Another cap of 120,000 immigrants from the Western Hemisphere was also put in place, with visas available on a first-come, first-serve basis. There was no cap placed on family reunification visas, which created a chain migration that allowed immigrants who attained citizenship to sponsor the immigration of adult relatives.

*President Lyndon B. Johnson signed the Hart-Celler Act in 1965, effectively removing immigration quotas.*

## PRESIDENT KENNEDY WEIGHS IN

"The famous words of Emma Lazarus on the pedestal of the Statue of Liberty read: 'Give me your tired, your poor, your huddled masses yearning to breathe free.' Until 1921 this was an accurate picture of our society. Under present law it would be appropriate to add: 'as long as they come from Northern Europe, are not too tired or too poor or slightly ill, never stole a loaf of bread, never joined any questionable organization, and can document their activities for the past two years.'"
—John F. Kennedy, 35th President of the United States

John F. Kennedy, *A Nation of Immigrants*. New York, NY: Harper and Row, 1964, p. 45.

After the passage of the Immigration and Nationality Act, immigration was once again on the rise. In the 1970s, 4.5 million people came to the United States, with Latinx making up 40 percent of the total. Another 5.6 million immigrants entered the country in the 1980s, and 11 million more came in the 1990s. These numbers include unauthorized immigrants; by 2015, about 11 percent of all immigrants were living in the country illegally.

The percentage of Latinx in the foreign-born population rose dramatically from the 1980s until about 2009, but it has almost stagnated over the past decade. Although immigrants still come to the United States from Europe, their numbers are but a fraction of what they once were. They lost their majority status among foreign-born people in the United States in the 1980 Census, signifying the end of an era of American immigration. As a new era of immigration began, the United States could no longer look to the past to predict what effect the immigrants of the 21st century would have.

# CHAPTER 2

# Immigration in the 21st Century

Today, there are more than 43 million immigrants living in the United States, accounting for about 13.5 percent of the country's population. Most come from Mexico, India, and China, although every country on Earth is represented somewhere in the United States. Immigrants come to the United States now for the same reasons they have come throughout its history: for better economic and social opportunities, and by extension, better lives. Over the past 50 years, however, immigration has boomed in America like never before. The United States attracts newcomers like a magnet; its labor-hungry, capitalist economy is in constant need of new workers, especially ones who are willing to work for minimum wage. Even this image of immigrants, though, is changing.

Contrary to popular belief, almost half of all immigrants work white-collar jobs, and although many still work in fields such as agriculture, food service, and construction, a growing number of immigrants are getting jobs in information technology, life sciences, and high-tech manufacturing. Since 2010, the number of college-educated immigrants allowed into the country has jumped from 29 to 44 percent, and they are now overrepresented in most science, technology, engineering, and math-related fields. The American economy, measured in terms of gross domestic product (GDP), which is the total value of all goods and services produced within the nation's borders, was $17.9 trillion in 2016, the largest in the world. Its growth is currently estimated at 2.1 percent annually, and that is in part due to the large number of skilled immigrants now making above-average income and paying higher taxes.

## Changes in the U.S. Census

The U.S. government has conducted a nationwide census to determine the size of the American population every 10 years since 1790. The valuable statistical information collected by the Census aids in the drawing of congressional districts and the distribution of federal and state money for social services. In 2010, changes in how the Census is conducted reflected the rapid growth of communities and ethnic groups in the United States, as well as the greater reliance by the government, community organizations, and businesses on the gathered data. The U.S. Census website explained:

*During previous decennial censuses, most households received a short-form questionnaire, while one household in six received a long form that contained additional questions and provided more detailed socioeconomic information about the population.*

*The 2010 Census will be a short-form only census and will count all residents living in the United States as well as ask for name, sex, age, date of birth, race, ethnicity, relationship and housing tenure—taking just minutes to complete.*

*The more detailed socioeconomic information once collected via the long-form questionnaire is now collected by the American Community Survey. The survey provides current data about all communities every year, rather than once every 10 years. It is sent to a small percentage of the population on a rotating basis throughout the decade. No household will receive the survey more often than once every five years.*[1]

1. "American Community Survey," U.S. Census Bureau. www.census.gov/history/www/programs/demographic/american_community_survey.html.

Despite all this, immigrants are often still treated poorly. Discrimination and racism play a daily part in an immigrant's life, putting them in difficult and even dangerous positions. Even though it is illegal to do so, employers and landlords may deny applications from immigrants based on their name or mode of dress. Hate groups such as the Ku Klux Klan (KKK) target them. In the case of unauthorized immigrants, they may be arrested and deported at any time and taken away from their families and friends. It has always been hard to be an immigrant in the United States, but as racial and political tensions rise, life for many immigrants in 21st-century America has become a harrowing experience.

## From Latin America

In 2011, the U.S. Census Bureau defined "Hispanic" or "Latino" as "a person of Cuban, Mexican, Puerto Rican, South or Central American, or other Spanish culture or origin regardless of race."[6] Latinx were the fastest-growing ethnic group in the United States until 2013 and still represent the largest minority in the country as almost 18 percent of the population. Immigration to the United States from Latin America has certainly aided in this growth; with 19.4 million people identifying as being of Latinx origin, about 35 percent of Latinx in the United States are foreign-born. As with most other immigrants, Latinx immigrants come to the United States mainly for economic reasons.

Mexico, for example, is a poor nation when compared to America, with a GDP of $1.1 trillion, a fraction of America's $18 trillion. The GDP per person in Mexico was only $9,000 in 2015, while the U.S. GDP per person averaged $55,800.

*Latinx immigrants often come to America to ensure a better future for their children.*

Despite recent economic growth, jobs in Mexico are scarce and pay little, and jobs in the United States in the farming, construction, and service industries are easier to come by. These occupations pay little compared to other jobs in the United States, but the salaries are frequently many times higher than what similar work would pay in Mexico.

## The Minority Shift

As the percentage of Chinese and Indian immigrants the United States takes in every year is beginning to outweigh that of Latinx immigrants, another shift in the ethnic makeup of the country is also taking place. Some predict that within the next half-century, the total number of minorities in America will outnumber non-Hispanic whites, making white people a minority in the country for the first time. An article in the *U.S. News & World Report* stated,

*According to the U.S. Census Bureau, in 2014 there were more than 20 million children under 5 years old living in the U.S., and 50.2 percent of them were minorities ...*

*... the number of minority and mixed-race children in the U.S are only expected to rise. "More than half of the nation's children are expected to be part of a minority race or ethnic group," by 2020, the U.S. Census Bureau reports, referring to all kids under the age of 18.*

*The minority population is expected to rise to 56 percent of the total population in 2060, compared with 38 percent last year. When that happens, "no group will have a majority share of the total and the United States will become a 'plurality' [nation] of racial and ethnic groups," the U.S. Census states. The minority-majority trend reflected among 5-year-olds is the beginning of that shift.*[1]

1.  Noor Wazwaz, "It's Official: The U.S. Is Becoming a Minority-Majority Nation," *U.S. News & World Report L.P.*, July 6, 2015. www.usnews.com/news/articles/2015/07/06/its-official-the-us-is-becoming-a-minority-majority-nation.

Although the Mexican minimum wage was increased at the beginning of 2016 to 73.04 pesos per day, or about 3.55 U.S. dollars (USD), the American federal minimum wage of $7.25 per hour is quite a bit more money, and some states set the minimum wage even higher than the federal standard. This disparity, or difference, has led many in Mexico to move to the United States with the hope of finding better jobs. Mexicans now account for approximately 64 percent of all Latinx, both foreign- and native-born, in the United States, making them the largest national group within the Latinx community.

Mexicans, as well as people from Latin American countries such as Guatemala and Honduras, travel to wherever jobs can be found within the United States, but they have traditionally migrated to major metropolitan areas in four states—California, New York, Texas, and Florida—which are now home to 14 million Hispanic immigrants, both authorized and unauthorized. Within these areas, Latinx immigrants have established large communities where the cultural traditions from their homelands are preserved.

## From Asia

In 2014, there were approximately 13 million Asian immigrants in the United States, the first 34 percent of which was made up of Indian and Chinese migrants, contributing 2.2 and 2.1 million people, respectively. India, China, the Philippines, Vietnam, and Korea account for the top 68 percent of Asian immigration, as well as one-fifth of the total foreign-born population in America. Most Asian immigrants come to America on family-sponsored visas, joining family members who are already native-born or naturalized citizens. Like Latinx immigrants, Asian immigrants come to the United States to build better lives for their families; in many Asian countries, overpopulation makes personal success difficult. "Asian countries are the most populous, [have] more competition and less resources," said Sean Luo, a first-generation American from China. "We are just being rational to immigrate to the countries where there are less people and more resources."[7]

Unlike most Latinx immigrants, many Asian immigrants are coming to America to go to school before looking for work.

According to a report by the Council of Graduate Studies, China, India, and South Korea lead international applications to American graduate schools. Because of the recent economic upturns in these countries, more and more young people can afford America's high tuition costs and are able to travel abroad to go to college. These young people then graduate and are recruited into the high-skill fields where they generally thrive.

*Many young Asian immigrants come to America for college.*

Although Asian immigrants are generally more well-received than their Latinx counterparts, many continue to feel estranged from American culture. According to the Pew Research Center, when asked if they felt like "typical Americans," 53 percent said no, and when asked if they felt they had been personally discriminated against in the past year, 19 percent said yes. Due to language and cultural barriers that can exist along with racism and cultural stereotypes, American society has been inept at reaching out to Asian immigrants despite taking them in for almost two centuries. Because of this, Asian immigrants are often segregated into "Chinatowns," "Little Tokyos," or "Little Indias," in much the same way that Latinx immigrants are, and the barriers are seldom broken down.

## Into American Cities

The growth of immigrant communities in the United States has led to a debate about the impact of mass immigration on America's urban centers. City dwellers across the United States consume vast amounts of water, food, electricity, and other items that must be carefully measured by urban planners to prevent shortages. Through the study of birth rates and the migration trends of the native-born population, planners can predict increasing and decreasing demand for a variety of systems necessary to successful urban management, such as water and sewage treatment, power supply, and transportation. However, it is difficult to meet the needs of cities with large immigrant communities because they grow faster than urban planners can account for and adapt to their needs.

The Federation for American Immigration Reform (FAIR), a national lobbying group that seeks improved border security and stricter controls on immigration, claims that these communities, which grow larger every year, are primarily responsible for urban sprawl, which is the unrestricted outward growth of cities that often harms the surrounding environment and puts a strain on natural resources: "For the sake of the environment, we must oppose immigration-driven population growth. Stopping America's rapid population growth is necessary for the sake of the environment and for the preservation of life for future generations."[8]

## PRESIDENT OBAMA'S REMARKS

"To this day, America reaps incredible economic rewards because we remain a magnet for the best and brightest from across the globe. Folks travel here in the hopes of being a part of a culture of entrepreneurship and ingenuity, and by doing so they strengthen and enrich that culture. Immigration also means we have a younger workforce—and a faster-growing economy—than many of our competitors. And in an increasingly interconnected world, the diversity of our country is a powerful advantage in global competition."

—Barack Obama, 44th president of the United States

Barack Obama, "Remarks by the President on Comprehensive Immigration Reform," speech, Washington, D.C., July 1, 2010. www.whitehouse.gov/the-press-office/remarks-president-comprehensive-immigration-reform.

Economically, however, immigration to large metropolitan areas may actually be helping the United States. As major centers of trade and culture, cities such as New York and Los Angeles are highly likely to host immigrant entrepreneurs once they have learned English and become citizens. Ted Hesson of *The Atlantic* stated,

> ... there is ample evidence that immigrants are creating businesses and revitalizing the U.S. workforce. From 2006 to 2012, more than two-fifths of the start-up tech companies in Silicon Valley had at least one foreign-born founder, according to the Kauffman Foundation. A report by the Partnership for a New American Economy, which advocates for immigrants in the U.S. workforce, found that they accounted for 28 percent of all new small businesses in 2011.

> ... immigration, on the whole, bolsters the workforce and adds to the nation's overall economic activity. Look at the impact on cities that attract the most foreign-born residents. New York, Los Angeles, Chicago, and Houston are all major immigrant destinations and also economic powerhouses, accounting for roughly one-fifth of the country's gross domestic product. In New York, immigrants made up 44 percent of the city's workforce in 2011; in and around Los Angeles, they accounted for a third of the economic output in 2007.[9]

Therefore, for as much as an increasing population may strain a nation's resources, immigrants tend to give back as much as they take.

Unfortunately, unauthorized immigrants are not allowed to contribute more to the society of their host country. The Center for Migration Studies estimates that there are about 10.9 million unauthorized immigrants in the United States, about half of whom are from Mexico, although the numbers have fallen every year for the past decade. Although unauthorized immigrants make up only about 3.5 percent of the U.S. population as a whole, politicians often use the number "11 million" to scare people into thinking the country is being overrun, causing significant alarm among U.S. lawmakers and citizens.

## Unauthorized Immigrants in America

Unauthorized immigrants tend to fall into one of two categories: those who cross the border undocumented and those who were admitted legally and have overstayed their visas. They are motivated to come to the United States for economic reasons, much like authorized immigrants, but there are additional factors that drive them to cross the border illegally or refuse to leave after their visas have expired. Applying for a work visa or citizenship in the United States is a complicated process that can involve long waits of months or even years. Many who wish to come to the United States to work would rather skip the bureaucracy because their principle desire is to make money, not become U.S. citizens. Most do not intend to stay in America indefinitely, though many end up doing just that. In some cases, they encourage family members to join them after they have established themselves, creating what is called a chain migration that adds to the number of unauthorized immigrants.

### "GET IN LINE"

"Many Americans wonder why all immigrants do not just come to the United States legally or simply 'get in line' if they are unauthorized. These suggestions miss the point: There is no line available for unauthorized immigrants and the 'regular channels' do not include them."
—American Immigration Council

"Why Don't They Just Get in Line?," American Immigration Council, August 12, 2016. www.americanimmigrationcouncil.org/research/why-don%E2%80%99t-they-just-get-line.

It is difficult to determine how many unauthorized immigrants there are in the United States, and estimates vary widely. The very nature of their undocumented status makes it difficult to locate and track them, and many do their best to maintain a low profile. The Census Bureau is not empowered by legislative mandate to ask the citizenship status of respondents, but recent estimates put the number at around 10.9 million unauthorized immigrants in the United States—the lowest it has been since 2003. For the past decade, 11 million has been the number accepted by the media and the federal government. Some dispute this estimate, although there is little research to back up such contrary claims. The National Association of Former Border Patrol Officers (NAFBPO), for example, claims there are 18 to 20 million unauthorized immigrants, but this claim was made in an open letter by the NAFBPO chairman, not in a scientific study.

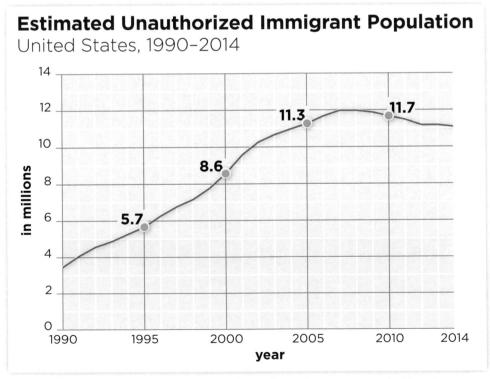

**Estimated Unauthorized Immigrant Population**
United States, 1990–2014

*Over the past decade, the number of unauthorized immigrants in the United States has leveled out, as this information from the Pew Research Center shows.*

With the media and politicians pointing fingers at Mexico as the source of illegal immigration, it is important to remember that not all unauthorized immigrants come from Mexico. Out of the 10.9 million unauthorized immigrants in America, only about 5.9 million are Mexican. The other 5 million is made up of people from El Salvador, Guatemala, India, Honduras, China, the Philippines, Korea, and many other countries. Although Mexicans make up over half of unauthorized immigrants, they are by no means the only ones in the country. Mexico, however, is unique in that it shares a border with the United States, making the United States the easiest country for Mexicans to get to, which is the simplest explanation as to why there is a disproportionate number of Mexicans in the unauthorized immigrant population. The Mexican-American border used to be very easy to cross, even though the journey was hazardous, and to many people looking for work, the rewards outweighed the risks.

## Crossing the Border

Although immigrants can be jailed and deported for being in the United States illegally, criminal enforcement of illegal immigration is a relatively recent phenomenon, arising mainly from concerns that unauthorized immigrants are putting a strain on government resources. Previously, the lack of immigration enforcement and poor security along the 2,000-mile (3,219 km) southern border allowed millions to come into the United States illegally without fear of being caught. Many who were arrested would disappear back into the population after being freed pending court hearings. In addition, government agencies in charge of tracking expired visas could not handle the backlog that developed with large numbers of immigrants, allowing unauthorized immigrants to continue living in the United States.

Getting caught and returned to their native country, however, is only one danger that unauthorized Mexican immigrants face. Crossing the border can be extremely hazardous, particularly in the summer months, when desert temperatures can reach higher than 110 degrees Fahrenheit (43 degrees Celsius). Every year, hundreds of immigrants die or suffer dehydration and heat stroke due to exposure. Dr. Samuel Keim, an associate professor of emergency medicine at the University of Arizona, created an index to inform unauthorized immigrants which days were the most dangerous for attempting a border crossing. "These people are dying on U.S. soil. This is a U.S. issue. It's not a Mexico issue," noted Keim. "If 100 people died anywhere in a single county from exposure, I think it would make national news."[10]

*Unauthorized immigrants are often caught right at the border and taken into custody by Border Patrol.*

The Mexican government issued an illustrated manual to notify border crossers of the dangers posed by the elements, and pro-immigration groups have voluntarily placed water stations along popular desert routes that unauthorized immigrants travel. Such actions have drawn criticism from groups that believe these actions only encourage illegal immigration. Barbara Coe, founder of the California Coalition for Immigration Reform, a political advocacy group that supports efforts to reduce immigration, stated, "That's called aiding and abetting. Illegal aliens are criminals. They can save their lives by staying home."[11]

*Along the Mexican-American border, signs warn Mexicans of the dangers of crossing the desert. This one reads, "Caution! Don't expose your life to the elements. It's not worth the penalty!"*

Unauthorized immigrants are also at the mercy of smugglers, referred to as "coyotes" by the U.S. Border Patrol. These smugglers take advantage of immigrants by charging high fees to aid them in crossing the border undetected. They have been known to leave border crossers lost in the desert or sell them into indentured servitude to dishonest business owners in the United States who force unauthorized immigrants to work and live in terrible conditions. There is little choice for immigrants in these situations because they fear that calling the police will lead to their own deportation.

## Education, Poverty, and Crime

Getting to America is a great ordeal for many immigrants, and many who arrive continue to face tough situations. Immigrants are often treated like criminals by the media and the government, making everyday life much harder for them. Most concerns about crime are directed at Latinx immigrants. However, that does not necessarily mean these concerns are warranted. The problem lies in a cyclical process that begins with education in Latin America.

In Mexico, for example, most primary and secondary education is statistically substandard—only 35 percent of children make it through high school—and only those in the upper classes can afford to send their children to good schools. This means the rich stay rich

and the poor stay poor because high-paying jobs generally require higher education. The poor then immigrate to America, and although the pay is much better than what they were making in Mexico, it is often minimum wage or lower, making social mobility as difficult as it was at home. Tuition at American colleges is prohibitively expensive, so few immigrants who find themselves in this position end up going back to school in order to find better employment.

*Although some Latin American schools, such as this one in Guatemala, are trying to revitalize their education system, many continue to struggle.*

## A FUTURE OF DEPORTATION

"I used to tell my students that they had to stay in school because eventually the laws would change, they would become citizens of this country, and they needed diplomas so they could make something of themselves as Americans. I don't tell them that anymore. Now I tell them they need to get their diplomas because an education will help them no matter what side of the border they're on."
—Ginette Cain, teacher at C. D. Hylton High School in Woodbridge, VA

Quoted in Ginger Thompson, "Where Education and Assimilation Collide," *New York Times*, March 14, 2009. www.nytimes.com/2009/03/15/us/15immig.html.

According to the Pew Research Center, in 2014, 17.7 percent of all foreign-born persons were living below the poverty level, compared to 14.5 percent of the native-born population. Among the foreign-born population living in poverty, Latinx made up the largest group, with 3.9 million impoverished immigrants. In American popular culture, poverty and crime are often related, so the media regularly paints the entire immigrant population, especially Latinx, as criminals, pointing to isolated incidents and making a commentary about immigrants as a whole. The fact is that immigrants in the United States have never been more likely to commit a crime than native-born people; they are statistically much less likely to be involved in criminal activity, as a report from the American Immigration Council shows:

*According to an analysis of data from the 2010 American Community Survey (ACS) ... roughly 1.6 percent of immigrant males age 18–39 are incarcerated [put in jail], compared to 3.3 percent of the native-born. This disparity in incarceration rates has existed for decades, as evidenced by data from the 1980, 1990, and 2000 decennial censuses. In each of those years, the incarceration rates of the native-born were anywhere from two to five times higher than that of immigrants.*

*The 2010 ACS also reveals that incarceration rates among the young, less-educated Mexican, Salvadoran, and Guatemalan men who make up the bulk of the unauthorized population are significantly lower than the incarceration rate among native-born young men without a high-school diploma. In 2010, less-educated native-born men age 18–39 had an incarceration rate of 10.7 percent—more than triple the 2.8 percent rate among foreign-born Mexican men, and five times greater than the 1.7 percent rate among foreign-born Salvadoran and Guatemalan men.*[12]

This does not, however, keep immigration policy from treating immigrants like criminals. With new policies directed specifically at immigrants in the name of safety, it is difficult for immigrants to remain innocent in the eyes of the law. For example, the Illegal Immigration Reform and Immigrant Responsibility Act (IIRIRA) broadened the definition of a felony only in the case of immigrants so they could be deported for crimes that are considered misdemeanors, or minor crimes, for the native-born population. This, in turn, takes away opportunities for immigrants to find better jobs, make more money, and go to school, which would make it easier to find better jobs in the first place and give immigrants the chance to rise above the poverty line and no longer be profiled as criminals.

This kind of cyclical process is called institutionalized oppression—a system of mistreatment toward any particular social group that is supported and enforced by society and social institutions. Although there is no reason that immigrants should not be able to achieve economic and social equality with native-born citizens in the United States, they are prevented from doing so simply because of their status as immigrants within the American cultural systems that keep them impoverished, poorly educated, and seen as criminals.

# CHAPTER 3

# Immigration and the Economy

Advocates of open immigration believe the high proportion of immigrant labor in the workforce has had a positive impact on the U.S. economy. By improving productivity, immigrant workers allow American businesses to grow, raising wages and increasing employment opportunities for people in complementary positions. On top of this, immigrants often open businesses of their own and create jobs. They also contribute by paying taxes; authorized or not, immigrants generally end up paying income, sales, and property taxes even if they do not file a tax return.

"Immigrants play an important part in the success of America's free-enterprise economy," noted Daniel Griswold, former director of Trade Policy Studies for the Cato Institute, a Washington, D.C., policy organization that engages in scholarly research and advocacy of legislative proposals. "They gravitate to occupations where the supply of workers falls short of demand, typically among the higher-skilled and lower-skilled occupations."[13]

Critics of immigration, however, say the benefits do not outweigh the costs resulting from the large number of unauthorized immigrants. While they use the same state and federal government services that citizens do, including public school education and medical and social welfare programs, some believe they pay no taxes, thus creating a net drain of government resources. Critics also believe immigrants take jobs away, filling positions that could have gone to native-born citizens—an unsupported theory.

## YOUNG IMMIGRANTS RAISE THE GDP

"This is a big advantage that the U.S. has over other countries—it is attracting the cream of the crop of scientific and technical talent from all over the world. If you segregated the groups into the highly skilled versus average [skilled], you would see the disproportionate contribution they make to GDP."
—Vivek Wadhwa, tech entrepreneur and author of *The Immigrant Exodus: Why America Is Losing the Global Race to Capture Entrepreneurial Talent*

Quoted in "What Migration Can (and Can't) Do for a Country's GDP," The Wharton School, September 9, 2013. knowledge.wharton.upenn.edu/article/what-migration-can-and-cant-do-for-a-countrys-gdp.

One area that is clearly creating a drain on government resources is the increased cost of securing the southern U.S. border and enforcing immigration laws that are being broken by unauthorized immigrants and the companies that hire them. Government representatives believe the increased security at the border and the stricter enforcement of immigration laws will decrease the amount the United States spends on immigrants, but the economic repercussions of kicking out and keeping out sources of tax money and labor remains to be seen.

## Taxes and Benefits

The federal and state governments raise the money required to provide public services and benefits to the population by collecting taxes on income and the manufacture and sale of goods and private services. The poor are heavily reliant on public services, but poor individuals and families generally pay less in taxes because their income and purchasing power are lower. Critics of immigration have drawn the conclusion that unauthorized immigrants who fall into this category use too many government resources.

A report published in May 2013 by the Heritage Foundation, a conservative policy organization, explained that the average unauthorized immigrant household in the United States received $24,721 in government benefits and services in 2010. These same households paid about $10,334 in taxes that same year, which led to a fiscal deficit of $14,387 that had to be picked up by other portions of the population. The implication of this article was that these immigrants are putting a severe strain on public resources.

This is an unfair characterization of impoverished immigrants. Native-born poor people in the United States also use more in services than they give back in taxes, since they caused a deficit of about $35,113 per household in 2010. There are also no statistics about the net deficit caused by the average immigrant family, as opposed to one with one or more unauthorized members.

## Immigration and Poverty

Some people argue that since many immigrants live below poverty level, the key to eliminating poverty in the United States is to limit immigration. Jared Bernstein, a senior fellow at the Center on Budget and Policy Priorities and former economist for the Obama administration, explained why this reasoning is faulty:

*Not unlike the analysis of single parents and poverty, too much analysis of this question basically argues that since immigrants, especially non-citizens (i.e., not naturalized) tend to be poorer than natives, if we take them out of the mix, we'd have less poverty. True: in 2012 (most recent data) the poverty rate for native-born persons was 14.3 percent while that of the foreign-born was 19.2 percent.*

*But that's not much of an insight. Since you could say the same thing about any group with below average incomes, it's pretty much saying we'd have less poverty if only we had fewer poor people.*[1]

1. Jared Bernstein, "Immigration and Poverty," *Huffington Post*, March 25, 2014. www.huffingtonpost.com/jared-bernstein/immigration-and-poverty_b_4650580.html.

Griswold pointed out that immigrants tend to be young and healthy and do not rely much on health care. Additionally, by law, unauthorized immigrants do not have access to unemployment benefits, food stamps, or Medicare. Griswold added that this assessment also does not take into account that second- and third-generation descendants typically make more money and achieve a better education than the foreign-born first generation, as determined in data collected by the U.S. Census Bureau.

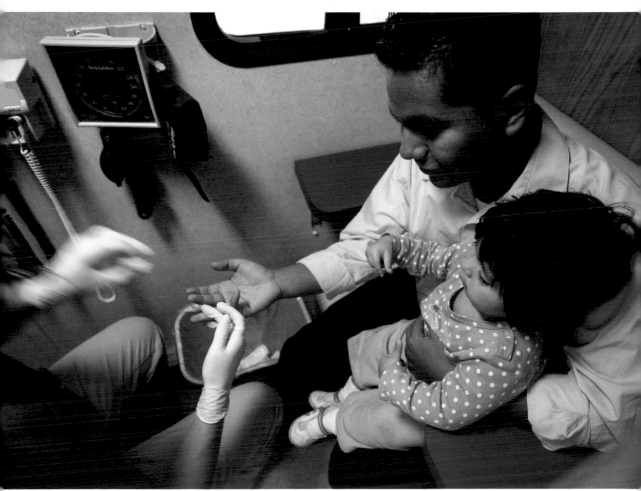

*Because they cannot apply for government health insurance, impoverished unauthorized immigrants in need of medical attention must go to free clinics or risk going into serious debt.*

## Unauthorized Taxpayers

Opponents of allowing unauthorized immigrants access to government services such as health care and education worry that the cost of these services is not being covered by the taxes these immigrants pay, giving them an unfair advantage by being allowed access to services paid for primarily by native-born and authorized immigrant taxpayers. Steven Camarota, director of research for the Center for Immigration Studies, a nonpartisan, nonprofit think tank that tends to lean anti-immigration, noted, "On average, the costs that illegal immigrant households impose on federal coffers [funds] are less than half that of other households, but their tax payments are only one-fourth that of other households."[14]

Immigration supporters disagree with this notion, arguing that the concept of allowing unauthorized immigrants access to social services is essentially making an investment in their current needs that will be paid back in the future through these immigrants' greater prosperity. Unauthorized immigrants also pay taxes because they are hoping to establish a paper trail that could one day lead to citizenship.

"I feel it's my responsibility to pay," said construction worker Dionicio Quinde Lima, an unauthorized immigrant in Queens, New York. "And if it helps me get papers, fine."[15] Lima and millions like him file income taxes with the Internal Revenue Service (IRS) with a taxpayer identification number that the IRS has given out since 1996 to encourage noncitizens—including unauthorized immigrants—to pay their taxes. In 2010, 3 million taxpayer ID card holders paid $870 million in income tax, and in 2012, unauthorized immigrants alone paid $11.8 billion in state and local taxes.

The IRS does not ask about citizenship status and does not care. "We want your money whether you are here legally or not," stated former IRS Commissioner Mark W. Everson, "and whether you earned it legally or not."[16]

In the last decade, unauthorized immigrants have paid around $100 billion into the government Social Security retirement fund that they will never be able to withdraw unless they become citizens, in which case they will be entitled to the benefits for which they have paid. This concerns some lawmakers because the Social Security fund is expected to run dangerously low with the impending retirement of 70 million Baby Boomers—people born between 1946 and 1964. They maintain that the additional withdrawals from previously undocumented immigrants that were not calculated into the fund's distribution could further drain the Social Security fund.

## PAVING THE PATH TO CITIZENSHIP WITH TAX DOLLARS

"They want to pay taxes because they want to be here and stay here and become U.S. citizens. They'll do whatever it takes, and they think it looks better on their behalf if they can prove they paid taxes. They think it will help them get some kind of permanent residency."
—Luis Diaz, former director of the service organization Progreso Latino

Quoted in Summer Harlow, "Filing Taxes Seen as Path to Citizenship," *Wilmington News Journal*, April 17, 2007.

Of further concern to lawmakers are the rising remittances, or cash payments, authorized and unauthorized immigrants send to relatives back home. In total, the United States sent out about $134 billion in remittances in 2015. Mexico alone received $24.3 billion. Critics of immigration resent remittances because they amount to money taken directly out of the U.S. economy for the benefit of other nations. However, remittances from America help grow the global economy by spreading out the wealth of the richest nation in the world and giving it to those that many need the money more, both on an individual level and an institutional one.

## Marketing to Latin Americans

Many in the business community believe immigrants do more good than harm for the economy. The large number of Latinx immigrants has led to exciting opportunities for companies looking to expand their consumer reach and increase their profits. In 2015, Latinx consumers added $1.3 trillion to the U.S. economy. That same year, Terry College's *Multicultural Economy Report* predicted that the spending power of the Latinx community could reach $1.7 trillion by 2020. Latinx-owned businesses in the United States are growing 15 times faster than the national average, and the total Latinx market in the United States ranks as the third largest Latinx economy in the world, following only the nations of Brazil and Mexico.

*Hispanic business owners often thrive in America.*

The desire for goods and services, as well as media entertainment in the Latinx community, has driven American companies to create consumer products and content that cater exclusively to its taste. In 2014, marketing agencies turned their attention to the growing Latinx economic influence and began devising strategies to successfully target this audience without estranging the rest of the country. Second- and third-generation immigrants, especially those who are part of the Millennial generation, became the focus of Latinx-centric marketing. Linda Lane Gonzalez, president of Viva Partnership, Inc., an independent ad agency that specializes in reaching the Hispanic market, said of Hispanic Millennials in a 2014 interview, "[T]hey're very proud of their Hispanic roots and their Hispanic culture, so they're maintaining a lot of traditions. At the same time, they live in both worlds, so they can live very biculturally. To get to their heart, you have to really understand that."[17]

## Do Not Assume

MP Mueller, the founder of advertising agency Door Number 3, offered some advice to people who want to market products to Latinx. On the *New York Times*' Small Business Blog, Mueller wrote,

*Learn some Spanish ... but don't assume that all Latinos want to be spoken to in Spanish—a mistake I've made. This goes for both advertising and personal interactions. Just because people appear to be Latino doesn't mean they want to be spoken to in Spanish. In fact, making that assumption can offend. If someone is having trouble understanding your English, ask, "Would you be more comfortable speaking in Spanish?" Even though your Spanish may be broken, the customer will feel good because you are making the effort. Come on, es facil [it's easy], it broadens you as a person and it will broaden your market, too.*[1]

This advice is relevant even for people who are not business owners. It is always better to ask than to assume what someone wants.

1. MP Mueller, "Marketing Tips for Reaching Hispanic Americans," *New York Times*, February 1, 2013. boss.blogs.nytimes.com/2013/02/01/marketing-tips-for-reaching-hispanic-americans.

## Immigrant Employment

Immigrants rarely come to America to be idle, which fits well in a country that takes pride in a strong work ethic. The latest wave of immigrants, though controversial, could not have come at a better time in America's economic development. Rising GDP, lowering unemployment rates, and the expanding markets of the global economy have created numerous opportunities for business owners and workers alike, and immigrants stand to benefit greatly from the prosperity.

Many immigrants have met the demand for low-skilled labor that the United States currently needs. The U.S. Bureau of Labor Statistics reported that of the top 30 jobs with the largest expected growth between 2014 and 2024, over half require "short-term-on-the-job" training. These jobs are typically in service industries and include retail sales, food preparation, landscaping, janitorial work, and home assistance. However, these jobs are not an ideal fit for the native population, where the median age of American workers is rising and more are attaining college degrees than ever before in the nation's history. These older and more educated workers are less likely to pursue low-wage jobs in the service sector that immigrants are more likely to accept.

## DEMAND AND SUPPLY

"It might seem intuitive that when there is an increase in the supply of workers, the ones who were here already will make less money or lose their jobs. Immigrants don't just increase the supply of labor, though; they simultaneously increase demand for it, using the wages they earn to rent apartments, eat food, get haircuts, buy cellphones. That means there are more jobs building apartments, selling food, giving haircuts and dispatching the trucks that move those phones. Immigrants increase the size of the overall population, which means they increase the size of the economy."
—Adam Davidson, founder of National Public Radio's "Planet Money"

Adam Davidson, "Debunking the Myth of the Job-Stealing Immigrant," *New York Times*, March 24, 2015. www.nytimes.com/2015/03/29/magazine/debunking-the-myth-of-the-job-stealing-immigrant.html.

There is concern among native-born, low-skilled workers who could be priced out of the job market by immigrants willing to work longer hours at tougher jobs for less money. The full impact that immigrant labor has on the ability of native-born Americans to get work is hard to gauge, since there is no way to accurately determine why someone does not get a particular job. However, there is little disagreement that companies will more readily hire workers who will work for less money because it means larger profit margins. It is also well established that immigrants who work for less money decrease wages in the industries they populate, and this has drawn the anger of many working-class citizens and labor unions that seek to protect workers' wages and benefits.

Recent studies, though, suggest that native-born and foreign-born workers are not competing for the same jobs. In an analysis released in 2015, the Urban Institute's Maria E. Enchautegui reported that native and immigrant workers without high school diplomas are very different from each other in the kinds of work they are able to do:

*These findings suggest that immigrants and native workers with low levels of education may be competing for different jobs and even could be complementing each other. Immigration status can*

Native-born and foreign-born Americans are not often competing for the same jobs.

*constrain a worker's job choices, but many immigrants are working
different jobs from natives because they have limited English language
or technical skills, or because they have insufficient exposure to the US
workplace. If undocumented immigrants become authorized to work in
the United States, that still may not be enough to increase competition
with natives for low-skilled jobs.*[18]

Native-born Americans in this category work as cashiers,
truck drivers, and janitors, while immigrants are more likely to
take jobs as housekeepers, cooks, and agriculture workers. While
some overlap does exist, and these are the places where arguments
for American workers' rights become legitimate, it would
appear that native-born Americans and immigrants are generally
not in competition with each other. Immigrants have also been
proven to create jobs by putting more demand on our economy.

## Unlawful Hiring

Despite the good that immigrants do for the U.S. economy, unauthorized
immigrants remain a sticking point—but due to little
fault of their own. Like authorized immigrants, unauthorized immigrants
will readily work for less money because it is still more
than they would receive for the same work in their native countries.
However, they are often taken advantage of by companies
that realize these workers generally do not know the rights and
benefits that all workers are entitled to by U.S. law and do not
report abuses for fear of being deported. These companies sometimes
find workers through equally unprincipled labor brokers
who seek out unauthorized immigrants and take part of their
salary as a fee for finding them the job. "The [guest worker] program
has been rife with abuses, even during the best of times,"
said Cindy Hahamovitch, a history professor at the College of
William and Mary. "There will never be enough inspectors to
check every labor camp, contract and field."[19]

Companies can only be penalized for hiring illegal workers if
they knowingly do so, which is difficult for prosecutors to prove
when a labor broker is involved because the company can claim
that it is the responsibility of the broker to establish a worker's citizenship
status. This behavior is especially common in the construction
industry, where many companies work through labor brokers.

*Construction companies hire unauthorized immigrants to do some of their most dangerous work but rarely compensate them appropriately.*

About 16 percent of unauthorized immigrants work in construction, making it the third most common job for the demographic. Their contribution to the industry is evident, but labor advocates have cited a high level of abuse. "These companies are getting rich on the backs of undocumented workers," noted Gustavo Maldonado, a union organizer with the Carpenters' District Council of Kansas City & Vicinity. "The workers are seen as the problem, but it's the companies that lure them to these construction jobs, pay them cash, or not pay them at all. It's not fair to the industry, and it's not fair to the workers."[20]

Construction companies, as well as companies in other industries that rely on cheap immigrant labor, reduce their costs by not offering wage and health benefits and by classifying their workers as independent contractors, which allows them to avoid checking immigration status and paying payroll taxes and workers' compensation. Additionally, legitimate businesses are at a disadvantage because companies that do not pay these benefits can offer their services at a lower price to public- and private-sector customers.

In 2006, the federal government began cracking down on companies that knowingly hired illegal immigrants. Highly publicized raids performed by Immigration and Customs Enforcement (ICE) in late 2006 and early 2007 led to arrest and deportation hearings for hundreds of unauthorized immigrants, and employers faced criminal penalties for hiring them. Since then, raids have become a seldom-used tactic in finding unauthorized immigrants and their employers, but they still take place. In Buffalo, New York, four Mexican restaurants owned by Sergio Mucino were raided in 2016. Mucino was arrested for harboring undocumented workers, as well as committing tax fraud by not reporting how much his restaurants earned.

## THE BEST OF WHAT WE EXPECT

"We're not talking about someone who just stepped off a bus and is asking for favorable treatment. We're talking about young students who exhibit the best of what we expect from all of our children: academic success and the desire to succeed even more."
–Donald E. Williams Jr., former Connecticut senator

Quoted in Stacy Stowe, "Bill Giving Illegal Residents Connecticut Tuition Rates Is Vetoed by the Governor," New York Times, June 27, 2007.

Punishing employers is widely believed by immigration reform advocates to help deter illegal immigration. If American companies face huge fines and the potential loss of their business, they will not readily hire illegal immigrants, which will dry up the job opportunities available. Those who continue to defend the hiring of unauthorized immigrants state the low wages they accept keep consumer prices down and generate healthy profits for American companies.

## The Cost of Homeland Security

Illegal immigration laws in the United States went largely unenforced for years. The number of people picked up illegally crossing the border was small in comparison to those who actually got through, and 98 percent of those arrested between 2000 and 2005 were never prosecuted, according to an Associated Press analysis of federal data. Security at the border has become of great concern since the terrorist attacks of September 11, 2001, when close to 3,000 people were killed by members of the Islamic terrorist group al-Qaeda. Members of al-Qaeda hijacked passenger planes and crashed them into New York's World Trade Center, the Pentagon outside of Washington, D.C., and a field near Shanksville, Pennsylvania. When it was revealed the terrorists responsible for the attack were all living in the United States illegally with expired student visas, it became apparent that America's immigration system was broken to the point of being a threat to national security. Policing the country's borders to prevent future attacks on American soil became a high priority for law enforcement.

No single fence lines either the Mexican or Canadian border. Borders are defined by a patchwork of fences, cameras, and sensors, and while government-employed agents patrol them, official border-crossing stations remain the most highly guarded parts. The Border Patrol website states,

> Often, the border is a barely discernible line in uninhabited deserts, canyons, or mountains. The Border Patrol utilizes a variety of equipment and methods to accomplish its mission in such diverse terrain. Electronic sensors are placed at strategic locations along the border to detect people or vehicles entering the country illegally. Video monitors and night vision scopes are also used to detect illegal entries. Agents patrol the border in vehicles, boats, and afoot. In some areas, the Border Patrol even employs horses, all-terrain motorcycles, bicycles, and snowmobiles.[21]

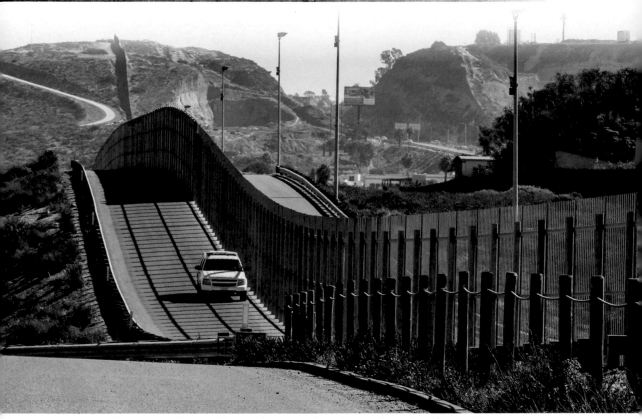

*Fences are only a small part of security along America's southern border. Cameras and motion sensors help Border Patrol officials guard places where effective fences are hard to build.*

Because of the length of America's borders—5,525 miles (8,892 km) of border with Canada and 1,933 miles (3,111 km) with Mexico—it is impossible to guard the whole thing at one time.

When Donald Trump campaigned for president, he promised to build one long wall across the entire border with Mexico. Some people supported this plan because they believed it would improve border security and stop the flow of illegal drugs and guns as well as unauthorized immigrants. However, others have opposed it, saying that such a wall would be too expensive to build and maintain, would not have any measurable effect on the illegal drug and gun trades, and would not halt most illegal immigration. Additionally, environmental workers have expressed concern about the problems a continuous wall would cause for plants and wildlife in the area.

At over $18 billion per year, the U.S. government's budget for immigration enforcement totals more than the budgets of most of its other prime law enforcement agencies combined. In 2012, the Border Patrol employed over 21,000 agents. With the lowest starting salary being $38,619 per year, the U.S. government is paying at least $811 million to staff of the Mexican and Canadian borders every year. Some of the rest is spent on the high cost of prosecuting unauthorized immigrants, of which there were 85,458 in 2012.

Operation Streamline is a project started in 2006 to arrest and convict, rather than deport, border crossers. It has swamped courts in the Southwest with immigration-related cases, spending tax dollars to incarcerate people who were once deported. About $1.87 billion was spent in

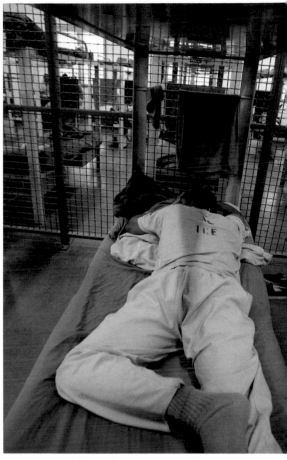

*Many unauthorized immigrants end up in federal detention centers such as this one, but maintaining them is expensive.*

2014 on the housing of imprisoned unauthorized immigrants, and $1.71 billion of that cost was shouldered by state taxes.

The debate about what level of responsibility for controlling immigration lies with the federal government versus with the states is ongoing. There is also a debate on whether the responsibility of assimilating immigrants into society lies with Americans or with the immigrants themselves.

# CHAPTER 4

# Adjusting to American Culture

American-born citizens, as well as newcomers from other countries, benefit from living together in the United States. Throughout U.S. history, great cultural adaptation took place when immigrants became part of the country's rich heritage. While immigrants gained access to the country's economic resources and were given the opportunity to improve their lives, native-born Americans gained the opportunity to enrich their own lives. Hot dogs, blue jeans, and many other things considered quintessentially American were absorbed from immigrants over the years, and Americans enjoy cuisine, music, and fashion from all over the world because of immigration.

The elements of this cultural exchange have changed over time with the addition of immigrants from different nations, but the principles of freedom, democracy, and individualism upon which the nation was founded remain unchanged.

## CULTURAL CHANGE GOES BOTH WAYS

"Change can be in more than one direction, of course, and many commentators on the American melting pot argue that its cultural content changes as new words become part of the common lexicon and new traditions penetrate mainstream popular culture."
—Jack Citrin, Amy Lerman, Michael Murakami, and Kathryn Pearson, social researchers

Jack Citrin, Amy Lerman, Michael Murakami, and Kathryn Pearson, "Testing Huntington: Is Hispanic Immigration a Threat to American Identity?," *American Political Science Association Perspectives on Politics*, vol. 5, no. 1 (March 2007): p. 32. www.ou.edu/uschina/gries/articles/IntPol/Citrin%20et%20al.2007.Testing.Huntington.pdf.

## Unaccompanied Minors

Since 2012, record numbers of child immigrants have crossed the Mexican-American border by themselves. Although their decision to come to the United States is the same, their demographics and histories vary widely:

*Although some have traveled from as far away as Sri Lanka and Tanzania, the bulk are minors from Mexico and from Central America's so-called Northern Triangle—Guatemala, Honduras, and El Salvador, which together account for 74 percent of the surge. Long plagued by instability and unrest, these countries have grown especially dangerous in recent years ...*

*Many of the kids are coming to help a family in crushing poverty. Some are trying to join a parent who left years ago, before the recession and increased border enforcement slowed down adult immigration. Still others are leaving because of violence from family members and gangs.*[1]

With no plan, many allow themselves to be picked up by Border Control to be put in government care while they go through the lengthy process of finding legal representation. With a lawyer, these children have a 50 percent chance of being allowed to continue their journey into the United States to find work or reunite with family. Without a lawyer, their chance is lower than 10 percent.

1. Ian Gordon, "70,000 Kids Will Show Up Alone at Our Border This Year. What Happens to Them?," *Mother Jones*, July/August 2014. www.motherjones.com/politics/2014/06/child-migrants-surge-unaccompanied-central-america.

Immigrants are expected to adopt and preserve these principles, as well as learn the English language and American customs in a process called assimilation. "Immigrants were expected only to abide by the basic tenets of an unspoken 'assimilation contract': allegiance to the nation's democratic principles, respect for individualism and hard work and—yes—willingness to learn English and use it outside their homes," wrote Peter D. Salins, professor of political science at the State University of New York at Stony Brook, in *Reinventing the Melting Pot*. "Beyond that, they were free to indulge ethnic, cultural or religious preferences and practices to their hearts' content."[22] Fears in the past that the assimilation contract that Salins refers to would be broken proved to be unfounded. Immigrants from many nations went on to become upstanding American citizens, even when native-born groups treated them with prejudice and attempted to prevent them from obtaining the rights of citizens.

Some believe the Latinx immigrant wave represents a challenge to this longstanding practice of assimilation. Opponents of open immigration fear the large numbers of Latinx coming to the United States will not assimilate, fracturing the unified national identity. Similar fears have been voiced about Muslim immigrants, especially in recent years. Many people believe they should be worried about Islamic extremists posing as immigrants or refugees in order to get into the country.

Supporters of immigration, however, maintain that Latinx and Muslim immigrants will assimilate in time like all immigrants before them and that it is too early to accuse them of breaking the assimilation contract. A 2007 Pew Research Center study found that "although many Muslims are relative newcomers to the U.S., they are highly assimilated into American society."[23] The study also found that the vast majority of Muslim immigrants reject Islamic extremism. Furthermore, immigration supporters believe it is native-born Americans who are in danger of breaking the contract if they push too hard for assimilation.

## The Evolution of American Identity

"Historically the substance of American identity has involved four key components: race, ethnicity, culture (most notably language and religion), and ideology,"[24] wrote Harvard professor Samuel P. Huntington in his book *Who Are We? The Challenges to America's National Identity*. While America's heritage of free enterprise and democracy and its cultural language component of English have remained unchanged throughout its history, the racial, ethnic, and religious elements have evolved over many years.

The American identity at the time of the Declaration of Independence could be described as white, Western European, and Protestant. This remained unchanged until after the Civil War, when two significant developments took place. Freed slaves were guaranteed basic civil rights by law, although institutionalized racism and segregation in the form of poll taxes, voting restrictions, and separate educational and health facilities kept blacks from achieving more equality for over a century. Also, the addition of Catholics from Ireland and Jews from Eastern and Southern Europe, as well as immigrants from Asia, began to change the religious, racial, and ethnic composition of the country. Though America remains 72 percent white in its racial composition, the evolution of its identity continues to this day.

*Many agree that a balance should be maintained between assimilation and preservation of one's culture. Pictured here is a girl dressed and ready for her quinceañera, the Latinx celebration of a young woman's 15th birthday.*

Huntington, a strong voice among opponents of open immigration, argued that American identity has not evolved but been deliberately changed in favor of a multicultural identity: "[Supporters of open immigration] encouraged immigrants to maintain their birth country cultures, granted them legal privileges denied to native-born Americans, and denounced the idea of Americanization as un-American."[25] In Huntington's view, the multiculturalism that these deconstructionists are trying to achieve will ultimately harm America's identity because it divides people. It does not offer the opportunity for celebrating the shared link of one overarching American identity, but instead encourages ethnic groups to derive strength from their differences.

## Equality and Justice for All

The Black Alliance for Just Immigration (BAJI) is a human rights organization advocating for the equality of black immigrants from Africa, the Caribbean, and Latin America. Since 2009, it has fought against racism and discrimination for one of the most overlooked groups of immigrants:

*BAJI educates and engages African American and black immigrant communities to organize and advocate for racial, social and economic justice. Local BAJI Organizing Committees in New York, Georgia, California and Arizona build coalitions and initiate campaigns among communities to push for racial justice. At the local and regional level, BAJI provides training and technical assistance to partner organizations to develop leadership skills, works with faith communities to harness their prophetic voice, and initiates vibrant dialogues with African Americans and black immigrants to discover more about race, our diverse identities, racism, migration and globalization. BAJI's flagship project is the Black Immigration Network (BIN), a national alliance that brings together black-led organizations and programs to advance just immigration policies and promote cultural shifts our communities need. The BIN kinship provides a safe, communal space for diverse black communities to connect, engage and advocate for equality and justice for all.[1]*

1. "Who We Are," Black Alliance for Just Immigration. blackalliance.org/who-we-are/.

Stanford University political science professor Luis R. Fraga and University of Washington political science professor Gary M. Segura contradicted Huntington's views and asked, "How important is a single national culture for the preservation of democratic institutions?"[26] In their view, multiculturalism gives groups the ability to maintain their ethnic and cultural heritage. They also cite examples of what they believe are successful democracies that have substantial ethnic and language diversity in Spain, France, and India. Some attest that each of these nations has suffered political conflict among various ethnic or religious groups that has led to violence: Spain was engaged in a decades-long conflict with Basque separatists until 2011, France continues its struggle to accept its Islamic population, and India has a history of religious conflict between Hindus and Muslims. However, it can be argued that anywhere cultures come together, there is bound to be conflict, but that fact does not make these places any less democratic or successful.

Generally, immigrants readily adopt American values, sometimes without realizing it. Boston College political science professor Peter Skerry noted they even adopt American perspectives on themselves: "Villagers from Mexico, Guatemala, Colombia and other Spanish-speaking countries do not come to the United States thinking of themselves as 'Hispanics' or 'Latinos.' That is an identity they acquire on these shores."[27] In other words, according to Skerry, people who make up the Hispanic community in the United States only think of themselves as Hispanic because they are in America. They campaign for civil rights and fair treatment in America based on an identity that is unique to the United States.

Despite their differing views on the virtues of the American identity in an age of multiculturalism, opponents of open immigration such as Huntington and supporters of open immigration such as Fraga and Segura do want the American identity to evolve in a way that benefits all Americans, immigrants and native-born alike. A balance must be maintained between the adoption of American culture and the preservation of the cultural elements brought by immigrants from their native lands.

## Latinx Are the New Germans

It is difficult to determine whether recent Latinx immigrants are actually assimilating into American society because assimilation is a process that takes place over generations, and many immigrants have not been in the United States long enough to be fully assimilated. Assimilation, or lack of it, can only be determined by comparatively measuring, among other things, the extent of English language usage and the economic status of U.S.-born children and grandchildren compared to that of their immigrant ancestors. Supporters of open immigration believe when opponents such as Huntington argue that Latinx are not assimilating, it is not only a premature assumption but also a false one. According to Gregory Rodriguez, writer and senior fellow of the pro-immigration group New America Foundation, Mexican-Americans have not attempted to build a parallel ethnic institutional structure and have never "shown much interest in distancing themselves from the mainstream ... For example, in Los Angeles, home to more Mexicans than any other city in the U.S., there is not one ethnic Mexican hospital, college, cemetery or broad-based charity."[28]

The concern Huntington and other opponents of open immigration express about the perceived lack of assimilation was commonly voiced in the past when large waves of German immigrants came to America in the 19th century. According to the 2010 Census, the Latinx population in the United States was 50.5 million, or 16 percent of the total U.S. population. By way of comparison, the number of people who claimed German ancestry in the 2013 American Community Survey was 49.2 million, or 15.6 percent of the total population. Germans living in America and Americans of German ancestry are almost equal in number to Latinx, yet there is no concern voiced by Huntington or any other advocates of controlled immigration about the high proportion of German-Americans in the United States. While much is heard about the issues and concerns of the Latinx community, there is no vocal German-American lobby that is petitioning for German rights, and there are no German-American leaders advocating German issues. Politicians and the media do not speak of the German vote, where Democrats and Republicans alike want the Latinx vote.

Harvard history professor Stephan Thernstrom maintains that the reason there is no German-American community that compares to the Hispanic-American community in terms of political action and visibility is because Germans have assimilated into American culture. "There was a German ethnic group once, a huge and powerful one," Thernstrom writes. "But having [ancestors] from Germany is not a significant indicator of how these people live and how they think of themselves."[29] During the high point of German immigration in the late 1800s, schools in Milwaukee, Wisconsin, which had the highest concentration of German immigrants in the country, taught students in German as well as English. Today, there are sizable German-American communities in cities across the United States, and there are festivals and parades in each of those cities that celebrate German heritage. However, that heritage is no longer the defining element of Americans of German descent living in the United States today.

*German festivals have become a yearly tradition in major cities across the country.*

## THE NATION SPEAKS

"The United States is not becoming a Spanish-speaking nation ... the facts do not support the increasing public image that millions of immigrants refuse to learn or speak English or do not want to assimilate."—Roberto Calderin, former chairman of the Orange County Human Rights Commission

Roberto Calderin, "Latino Immigrants Do Assimilate and Learn English," *Times Herald-Record* (Middletown, NY), October 5, 2006. www.recordonline.com/article/20061005/OPINION/610050311.

Evidence suggests that Latinx will eventually follow in the footsteps of the Germans. While cultural heritage remains important, many second-generation immigrants never learn to speak Spanish. Although some encourage their children to learn the language, English quickly becomes the norm in immigrant households after more than one generation has grown up in America. "The newest generations of immigrants are assimilating into American society as fast and broadly as the previous ones," Julia Preston of the *New York Times* wrote in an article about the newest report on immigrant acculturation, "with their integration increasing over time 'across all measurable outcomes.'"[30]

Like the German immigrants in the 1800s, Latinx immigrants tend to concentrate in certain areas; California, New York, Texas, and Florida are destinations of choice because they already have large Latinx populations. Ethnic enclaves, which are communities made up of distinct ethnic groups, are not unique in the immigrant experience, since strangers in a strange land will often gravitate toward what is familiar to feel safer. However, no other immigration wave has had such a high percentage of people who speak the same language, and the large populations in the Latinx enclaves add to the concern that assimilation will be slowed or not take place at all.

People concerned with the lack of assimilation among Latinx immigrants believe that within these tight-knit communities, where all the basic necessities of life can be provided by familiar faces speaking Spanish, there is little need to reach out and interact with the broader population. The regional concentration of immigrants may be changing, though, as statisticians—people who study statistics—have noted immigrants dispersing to other areas, suggesting that Latinx immigrants are integrating into and becoming accepted in traditionally native-born American communities.

A further positive sign that assimilation is taking place is the rising level of American identity among Latinx. A 2002 Pew Research Center survey that inquired how Latinx preferred to identify revealed that while only 7 percent of foreign-born Latinx identified first as Americans, 31 percent of second-generation Latinx and 56 percent of third-generation Latinx identified primarily as American.

*Mexican immigrants strive to find a balance between their traditions and their new life in the United States.*

## Becoming a Citizen

For documented immigrants, becoming an American citizen mainly consists of jumping through the government's hoops. "To become a U.S. citizen," the *Washington Post* explained, "a legal permanent resident must be at least 18; have lived in the United States continuously for five years; be able to speak, read, write and understand basic English; pass a background check; demonstrate knowledge of U.S. government and history, and swear allegiance to the United States."[31] Becoming a citizen gives immigrants the right to vote and to receive aid from government programs such as unemployment and Medicare, and it also ensures that they cannot be deported. Their children, too, will be citizens, even if they are born in another country.

*The final step to becoming a U.S. citizen involves an oath ceremony where naturalized immigrants pledge allegiance to their new country.*

As of 2014, 20 million immigrants in the United States have become naturalized citizens—about 47 percent of all immigrants in the country. Among the countries of origin with the highest rates of naturalization are Vietnam, Russia, the Philippines, and Korea, with Mexico, Guatemala, and Honduras among those with the lowest. When asked why they do not become citizens, many authorized Mexican immigrants expressed worries about not being proficient enough in English and failing the citizenship test, as well as about the $680 application fee. Twelve percent, however, said they just had not gotten around to it.

## A NATION OF IMMIGRANTS

"Work ethic, human rights values, value of education have all been imported throughout America's cultivation as a young nation. Many around the world still look to America as a place they want to come—and give everything they have to offer. We should ask ourselves what it is that made America great in the first place before we decide what we can do to make it better."
—Aymann Ismail, video producer and editor for *Slate* magazine

Aymann Ismail, "What Assimilation Problem, Donald?," *Slate*, March 7, 2017. www.slate.com/articles/news_and_politics/politics/2017/03/the_white_house_s_beliefs_about_muslim_assimilation_are_completely_bogus.html.

## Learning English

While Latinx have a comparatively lower tendency toward naturalization than other immigrant groups, by and large they are following traditional patterns of absorbing the English language. Generally, immigrants follow a pattern in which the foreign-born first generation overwhelmingly speaks the native language while having little mastery of English. The second generation demonstrates a mastery of English and is generally bilingual (speak both English and their native language), and the third generation speaks English almost exclusively with little, if any, use of their native language. A study of two decades' worth of Census data by University of California, Berkeley, professors

Jack Citrin, Amy Lerman, Michael Murakami, and University of Minnesota professor Kathryn Pearson determined that "Mexican immigrants may know less English than newcomers from other countries when they arrive in the United States, but … their rate of linguistic assimilation [the rate at which they learn English] is on par with or greater than those of other contemporary immigrant groups."[32]

*Most immigrants find that learning basic English makes it easier to fit into American culture, so they take English as a Second Language (ESL) classes such as this one.*

According to a 2011 Pew Hispanic Center report, 61 percent of first-generation Hispanic immigrants had Spanish as their primary language, and 62 percent did not speak English very well. The second generation demonstrated a marked improvement in English language ability, with 8 percent speaking only Spanish or more Spanish than English, 53 percent speaking Spanish and English equally, and 40 percent speaking only English. By the third generation, 69 percent considered English to be their primary language, and only 47 percent could speak Spanish well. This level of change in only one generation shows there is little need for concern about the prevalence of Spanish-language media and advertising affecting linguistic assimilation in the United States. It also comes as welcome news for Hispanics looking to get ahead in the job market. "Hispanic immigrants who speak English earn 17 percent more than those who do not," noted Harvard University professor George J. Borjas, "even after adjusting for differences in education and other socio-economic characteristics between the two groups."[33]

## The Language of Education

In order for immigrant children to have the tools they need to succeed later in life, it is essential that they learn to speak English proficiently. However, there is an ongoing debate as to the best way to teach English in America's public schools, with supporters of bilingual education squaring off against supporters of English language immersion.

Bilingual education is a program that starts out by teaching elementary school students in their native language, with gradually increased exposure to English as they move through the school system. Supporters of bilingual education claim it allows children to gain literacy and fundamental knowledge in subjects such as math and science in their native language before tackling English literacy and proficiency. It is also believed that this program avoids subjecting children to the psychological trauma of isolation from their English-speaking classmates and prevents them from getting behind in other school subjects while maintaining cultural ties to their native heritage.

English language immersion is a program in which children are taught English from an early stage in their educational development. They are also instructed in the fundamentals of math and science in English, thereby allowing them to achieve English proficiency at a faster rate. Supporters of English language immersion note that students more readily grasp both English and other subjects, and they assimilate faster than they would with bilingual education.

The California public school system, which has more Hispanic students than any other school system in the country, has experimented with both programs, and there are teachers and parents who passionately support one program or the other. However, a five-year study by the California State Legislature found no conclusive evidence that either program was more effective than the other. As with many other aspects of the larger debate on immigration, no single answer can be applied to the entire immigrant community.

*Whether through bilingual education or English language immersion, it is important for immigrant children to be taught English early. After age seven, language learning becomes more difficult.*

# The Future of Immigration

t has been more than 50 years since the federal government made any fundamental change in immigration policy. The 1965 Hart-Celler Act eliminated the national origin quotas that had been in place for decades. Although national security became top priority after the September 11, 2001, terrorist attacks, with the creation of the Department of Homeland Security (DHS), which took over the enforcement of immigration policy, the only thing that changed about the immigration system was its size. More border guards were hired and borders were more carefully watched, but nothing was significantly improved in the eyes of either the pro- or anti-immigration crowds.

During the Obama administration, the country's immigration policy was finally enforced, and it resulted in the removal of about 2.9 million people, the most deported under any president. The majority of these people were apprehended directly at the border, the place where most of the enforcement was concentrated, and instead of simply being informally tossed back over the way they had been for so long, they were arrested and formally deported. Obama's immigration enforcement was controversial because of the amount of money it cost to formally prosecute unauthorized immigrants, as well as because of what seemed to be racial profiling happening in immigrant investigations in the interior.

Stirring up more controversy was the Deferred Action for Childhood Arrivals (DACA) program. This program protects unauthorized immigrants brought into America as children by their parents, taking into account that they did not choose to immigrate illegally. It was created through an executive order—a document issued by the president that functions as a law—signed by Obama when Congress did not pass the Development, Relief, and Education for Alien Minors (DREAM) Act. The DREAM Act is a law that, if passed, would have helped unauthorized immigrants get important documents such as work permits, a Social Security number, driver's license, and green card (authorization to stay in the country on a long-term basis). The DACA program prevents children of unauthorized immigrants, sometimes called "DREAMers" because of the DREAM Act, from being deported and gives them the right to apply for the same documents as the DREAM Act, with the exception of a green card. DACA is not popular among conservatives, even though it does not grant citizenship or even promise a path to citizenship.

Despite the recent administrative attempts to fix America's current immigration policy, neither side of the argument has been appeased. Conservatives want to see stricter laws put in place to deport and keep immigrants out of the country, while liberals want to see immigrants welcomed and no longer unnecessarily criminalized. Both sides wish to see major reform in the future, but how to get there—and how to agree—remains in question.

## The 2016 Election

Although Democrats and Republicans agree that maintaining national security and fixing the economy are of the utmost importance, they have vastly different opinions about how those goals should be accomplished with regard to immigration. Democrats tend to lean liberally, pushing for more open immigration policies to stimulate the economy, as well as fighting to end unnecessary separation of mixed-status families and to create a path to citizenship for unauthorized immigrants. Republicans tend to lean conservatively, working to stop the flow of immigration from less prosperous nations and remove as many unauthorized immigrants from the United States as possible. With such contrasting views, Democrats and Republicans often work against each other, aggressively blocking each other's policies in Congress and making government reform stagnate. Because of recent deadlock and frustration on both sides, the immigration debate became one of the main points of contention during the 2016 presidential campaign, aggravating the growing divide between parties. While immigration has been a deciding topic before, candidates have rarely been so polarized, or divided.

Democratic presidential nominee Hillary Clinton focused on immigrants as individuals rather than a group and promised comprehensive plans to "fix the family visa backlog, uphold the rule of law, protect our borders and national security, and bring millions of hardworking people into the formal economy."[34] Supporting a path to citizenship, Obama's DACA program, welcoming refugees, and ending private immigrant detention centers, Clinton represented a very liberal mindset when it came to immigration. She also held the view that only immigrants who had a history of violence or criminal activity should be deported. This view, while well-intentioned, led some to worry about a broadening of the definitions of "violent" and "criminal" only when used to categorize unauthorized immigrants. It was thought by some that Clinton would have had to make changes in those definitions to shake the accusations of profiling, but her overall immigration policy was pleasing to most Democrats.

*Hillary Clinton appealed to Latinx voters because of her open stance on immigration and immigrant rights.*

Republican presidential nominee Donald Trump fell on the opposite side of the spectrum, with extremely conservative views on immigration. In the name of national security, Trump proposed constructing an impenetrable wall between the United States and Mexico, ending the DACA program, and shutting down all immigration from predominantly Muslim countries. He also promised to deport all unauthorized immigrants. When Trump was elected president, many authorized and unauthorized immigrants worried about their futures.

*Donald Trump appealed to many voters because of his strong views on immigration reform.*

## ENDING THE POLITICS OF DIVISION

"Despite the central role they play in our economy and in our daily lives, undocumented workers are reviled by many for political gain and shunted into the shadows. It is time for this disgraceful situation to end. It is time to end the politics of division on this country, of politicians playing one group of people against another: white against black, male against female, straight against gay, native born against immigrant."

—Bernie Sanders, Vermont senator and former presidential candidate

Bernie Sanders, "Prepared Remarks for National Association of Latino Elected and Appointed Officials Conference," Bernie 2016, June 19, 2015. berniesanders.com/naleo-conference-remarks.

## ICE and Deportation

U.S. Immigration and Customs Enforcement (ICE) was founded in March 2003 by the then-new DHS, replacing the Immigration and Naturalization Service (INS). According to the ICE website, the agency "enforces federal laws governing border control, customs, trade and immigration to promote homeland security and public safety."[35] ICE is known for its extensive raids, the results of which have been about 1.5 million deportations from the interior during the Obama administration. Primarily going after unauthorized immigrants who have missed deportation hearings, those with connections to terrorist organizations, and those with criminal records, ICE works to remove immigrants who may be threats to national safety.

## THE FEAR OF DEPORTATION

"To be honest with you, I'm scared. How can they just pluck me out of my family, my kids? If they can do this to me, they can do it to anybody."

—Zoila Meyer, former Adelanto, California, city councilmember threatened with deportation because she never became a citizen

Quoted in Robert Jablon, "Ex-SoCal Councilwoman Could Be Deported," *Washington Post*, June 24, 2007.

*ICE is known for raiding businesses it suspects may be employing undocumented immigrants.*

Critics of the organization, however, believe many of the deportations that have taken place were not warranted. Some worry about the grounds on which unauthorized immigrants are arrested and deported, claiming that many are deported on technicalities and without regard for individual circumstances:

> *As proof that it is weeding out the "bad guys," Immigration and Customs Enforcement (ICE) recently reported that 59 percent of deportations in fiscal [financial] year 2013 [October 2012–September 2013] involved noncitizens with criminal records. Yet, what ICE did not highlight is that the vast majority of criminal deportees were expelled for non-violent offenses, with 60 percent convicted of misdemeanors punishable by less than one year in prison …*

## Unable to Be Heard

They make up a significant portion of America's population, but noncitizen immigrants and unauthorized immigrants are unable to vote because they are not U.S. citizens. Although this is standard practice in every country around the world, it can make it difficult for a significant number of people who are affected by government policy to make their voices heard. While citizen advocates have tried to make changes on their behalf, frustration with the system boiled over on October 26, 2016, 18 days before the presidential election. Protesters for immigrant voting rights chained themselves together across the George Washington Bridge going into New York City. Protestor Mahoma Lopez explained, "Just basically to tell the system we're not going to be in the shadows anymore. We are here and we contribute to the community, we pay taxes, and we consume ... The majority of immigrant people, we don't have the right to vote."[1] Even though their wishes to be given the vote will not be granted unless they become citizens, they still wanted to make their voices heard in some way.

1. "Protesters Disrupt Traffic on George Washington Bridge, Cause Major Delays," CBS Local Media, October 26, 2016. newyork.cbslocal.com/2016/10/26/george-washington-bridge-protest.

*"Smart enforcement" strategies have led to an unprecedented level of cooperation between ICE, the FBI ... and local police agencies as they seek to target "terrorists" and "criminal aliens." Not surprisingly, the proportion of criminal to non-criminal deportations has grown steadily [over] the past decade. Yet, we have seen national declines in crime rates over the same period, and studies have shown that immigrants are much less likely than US citizens to commit crimes. Immigrants are not becoming more unlawful or dangerous; the government is just more aggressive in labeling them as such.*[36]

Some advocates for immigrant rights maintain that these raids are just excuses to conduct mass deportations of hardworking people who are immigration violators but do not pose a danger to the public. "They're trying to sell it as something where they target (criminals) but it's become part of a larger dragnet,"[37] said Pedro Rios, director of the American Friends Service Committee in San Diego, California.

Immigrant arrests that break up families have also been a focus of concern. In 2010, the Pew Hispanic Center estimated there were 9 million people living in mixed-status families in the United States where at least one member was in the country illegally. Raids that round up immigration violators have the potential to take fathers and mothers away from their children, and vice versa. In these situations, unauthorized immigrants have the right to make their circumstances known to immigration judges, who make the final decision about whether or not to deport individuals. Due to an extensive case backlog, potential deportees can remain in legal limbo for months, which creates an agonizing emotional situation while their fates are decided.

By definition, all unauthorized immigrants have, in fact, broken the law because they are violators of immigration

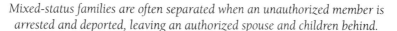

*Mixed-status families are often separated when an unauthorized member is arrested and deported, leaving an authorized spouse and children behind.*

regulations. Pro–immigration-control groups believe it is unfair to allow unauthorized immigrants opportunities available to authorized immigrants and citizens who have obeyed all the laws, including immigration regulations. However, since the vast majority of unauthorized immigrants are otherwise law-abiding people whose only desire is to find better jobs than were available in their native countries, many supporters of immigration are willing to forgive their violations. They also do not see the reason for the nationwide sweeps being conducted by ICE. In their view, if immigrants are working hard and obeying the law, they should be afforded some of the rights available to citizens because they are contributing to the prosperity of the American economy.

However, President Trump's focus is on deporting un-authorized immigrants, rather than giving them citizenship. With a proposed 40,000 new agents, tripling its current force, ICE could conduct even more deportation raids, separating more families and flooding the court and prison systems with unauthorized immigrants.

## Sanctuary Cities

*The Economist* defined sanctuary jurisdictions as "American cities, counties or states that protect undocumented immigrants from deportation by limiting cooperation with federal immigra-tion authorities. Some decline to use city or state tax dollars to enforce federal immigration laws. Many prohibit local officials from asking people about their immigration status."[38] In the United States, many major cities are sanctuary cities, which do not report undocumented immigrants to the federal govern-ment when they are arrested and charged. Many cities made this decision because they realized that when immigrants were de-ported after being arrested for minor crimes, the trust between police and immigrant communities was broken. The threat of being deported kept unauthorized immigrants from reporting crimes, creating a bigger public safety risk than what most im-migrants were being charged with—mainly traffic violations and other nonviolent misdemeanors. Among the sanctuary cities in America are New York, Boston, Chicago, Seattle, New Orleans, San Francisco, and Los Angeles, as well as many others.

*New York City, the most populated city in the United States, is a sanctuary city.*

This pushback from local governments started after the institution of Secure Communities under President George W. Bush. This was a program that allowed ICE to file requests with city police departments to hold unauthorized immigrants for up to 48 hours after they were meant to be released in order for ICE to pick them up and begin the deportation process. Although some agreed to participate, many jurisdictions refused. Detaining people beyond their release date is a human rights violation, and there was outcry from immigrant communities regarding the suddenness of the deportations, which often happened with no notice to an immigrant's family. Secure Communities was scaled back in 2014, but in July 2015, the DHS introduced the Priority Enforcement Program (PEP), which was meant to replace Secure Communities. Unlike Secure Communities, PEP requests

48 hours' notification before an unauthorized immigrant's release from jail—and only in the cases of those convicted (found
guilty), not those who were only charged (accused). These
changes were meant to avoid public scrutiny, but immigration advocates continue to question the program's motives and
methods, and city governments continue to refuse to cooperate.

Trump has vowed to defund sanctuary cities to force them
to comply. This would leave major cities across the country with
no budget with which to fund social services. City government
officials, however, doubt he would make such a move. New
York City alone stands to lose $10.4 billion, but the mayors of
several cities have stated that they will not be giving up their
unauthorized immigrants. "They will make a choice that this is
not the battle they want to take on because they have bigger fish
to fry,"[39] determined Rahm Emanuel, Chicago's mayor.

## Sharia Law

With the Islamic extremist group Islamic State of Iraq and Syria (ISIS) terrorizing the Middle East and the rest of the world, politicians and media outlets have begun discussing Sharia law—the law according to the Qur'an—the holy book of Islam. ISIS claims to uphold this law, using it as justification for the torture, mutilation, and murder of nonbelievers, a fact that has caused concern among some because of the large number of Muslim immigrants America takes in. Since Sharia law is Islamic law, some people reason, and ISIS commits atrocities in the name of Sharia law, then Islam must be an evil religion. Some even fear that Muslim immigrants will follow Sharia law rather than the laws of the United States. However, all of these assumptions are false. ISIS does not interpret Sharia law the way most Muslims do; instead, the group uses it to falsely justify its evil actions. Carol Kuruvilla, an associate religion editor for the *Huffington Post*, explained,

*Sharia ... encompasses both a personal moral code and a general religious law that can influence the legal systems of Muslim-majority countries. It's also a living body of law—it developed over the centuries and is still being examined with fresh eyes by Muslim scholars and believers today ...*

*[Scholar Qasim] Rashid writes, "The most 'Muslim country' in the world is likely America, because America guarantees freedom of religion, freedom of speech, freedom of expression and freedom of thought—all hallmarks of Shariah Law. Those nations that oppress in the name of Shariah are as justified in their claims, as the slave owners who claimed their right to slavery was based on the Bible."*

*You do NOT need to worry about Sharia dominating American life and courts. Because nothing trumps the U.S. Constitution. No national Muslim organization has ever called for Sharia to supercede American courts. It's completely beside the point of Sharia and it's not something American Muslims want.*[1]

1.  Carol Kuruvilla, "5 Things You Need to Know About Sharia Law," *Huffington Post*, July 15, 2016. www.huffingtonpost.com/entry/5-facts-you-need-to-know-about-sharia-law_us_5788f567e4b03fc3ee507c01.

## The Conflict in Syria and the Conflict in Congress

While Latin American immigration remains at the forefront of current social debates, immigration policy being debated in Congress is mostly focused on a different group: Middle Eastern refugees, especially those from Syria.

The number of immigrants in the United States from the Middle East and North Africa region has doubled since the beginning of the new millennium due to the unstable political climate there, and as the situation worsens, more people seek safety every day. At the beginning of 2011, civil war broke out in Syria, forcing thousands of Syrians into Jordan, Iraq, Lebanon, Turkey, Egypt, and eventually Germany, Sweden, and the United Kingdom. By the end of 2016, with the war escalated by the terrorist organization Islamic State of Iraq and Syria (ISIS), 4.8 million people had been displaced from their homes, fearing for their lives. In October 2015, the Obama administration set a goal of taking in 10,000 refugees over the course of the fiscal year, a goal which it met a month early in late August 2016.

*Many Syrians travel to the United States and Europe to escape the civil war in their home country. These refugees often have little money and few possessions.*

Even before the United States responded to the crisis in Syria, fear in America slowed the process of refugee immigration to a crawl. During a Senate Homeland Security Committee hearing, Anne C. Richard, assistant secretary for the Bureau of Population, Refugees, and Migration, described the refugee screening system:

> All refugees of all nationalities considered for admission to the United States undergo intensive security screening involving multiple federal intelligence, security and law enforcement agencies, including the National Counterterrorism Center, the FBI's Terrorist Screening Center, and the Departments of Homeland Security, State and Defense. Consequently, resettlement is a deliberate process that can take 18-to-24 months.

> Applicants to the U.S. Refugee Admissions Program are currently subject to the highest level of security checks of any category of traveler to the United States. These safeguards include biometric (fingerprint) and biographic checks, and a lengthy in-person overseas interview by specially trained DHS officers who scrutinize the applicant's explanation of individual circumstances to ensure the applicant is a bona fide refugee and is not known to present security concerns to the United States.[40]

On top of this, however, conservatives believe that further measures should be taken to protect against outside threats.

Three new bills have been introduced to Congress since the beginning of the Syrian refugee crisis, each with the intent of limiting America's Syrian refugee intake. The first, the American SAFE Act of 2015, would require further FBI verification of any "covered alien"—a term that here means a resident of Iraq or Syria—wishing to enter the country as a refugee. "Individuals cannot be admitted as refugees until the FBI director certifies to the Secretary of Homeland Security and to the National Intelligence director that background investigations sufficiently determined they are not a threat to national security," explained political fact-checking website PolitiFact. "A refugee may also only be admitted after the Secretary of Homeland Security—in unanimous agreement with the directors of the FBI and National Intelligence—certifies to 12 'appropriate Congressional Committees' that the person is not a national security threat."[41]

This would make coming into America an even longer and more difficult process than it already is. The second, the Give States a Chance Act of 2015, would allow state governors to refuse Syrian refugees if they are not reasonably satisfied that the refugees are not security threats, but it would also create a loophole that would make it possible for governors to refuse refugees for no reason at all. The third and final bill, the Resettlement Accountability National Security Prioritization Act of 2016, would shut down all refugee admissions from Afghanistan, Iraq, Libya, Somalia, Syria, and Yemen. These bills, though, are still in Congress and may never see the president's desk to be signed into law.

## TOO IMPORTANT TO WAIT

"The issue of immigration is too important for our elected officials to abandon. It cannot wait for several more years. Human beings are suffering and dying."
—Gerald R. Barnes, Catholic bishop

Robert Pear, "Broad Effort to Resurrect Immigration Bill," *New York Times*, June 16, 2007. www.nytimes.com/2007/06/16/washington/16immig.html

## A Ban on Immigration

On January 27, 2017, Trump signed an executive order that included a 90-day ban on immigration from certain countries and a 120-day suspension of the U.S. Refugee Admissions Program (USRAP). This travel ban became known as the "Muslim ban" because it affected people from seven countries where Islam is the main religion. The executive order never specifically mentioned the word "Muslim," but it did say that after the ban was lifted, the DHS would "prioritize refugee claims made by individuals on the basis of religious-based persecution, provided that the religion of the individual is a minority religion in the individual's country of nationality."[42] Since Islam is the majority religion in the affected countries, the order does mean that non-Muslims would be given preference. This has caused many people to call the travel ban unconstitutional, since the United States has separation of church and state, which means laws are not supposed to be made that give preference to any one religion.

The executive order was controversial in other ways as well. Critics called it racist and shared stories on social media of Syrian children—even those who had passed all the necessary entry requirements—in need of medical care who were sent back to their war-torn country. They also opposed it because it affected people with visas and green cards—people who had already been approved to live and work in the United States. Some people with green cards who were out of the country when the ban went into effect had difficulty getting back in and had to go through extra security screenings, although the DHS promised that no one would be denied entry if the extra screenings did not reveal a history of terrorism.

The American Civil Liberties Union (ACLU) called the travel ban a violation of people's rights and requested a stop to the executive order. U.S. District Court Senior Judge James L. Robart granted the request on February 3, 2017, which meant the order was no longer being enforced at the country's borders; people from the specified countries were free to continue entering the United States. As of June 2017, the executive order is still being debated, but the Supreme Court lifted some of the restrictions on the executive order, allowing some parts of the ban to be enforced. The Supreme Court will also hear arguments on the travel ban, but court cases often take a long time to be resolved.

## Racism in America

Although many claim that immigration issues are purely economic, race and religion play a role as well. America has a long history with prejudice and racism, and while some think that racism is no longer a concern, racially fueled politics continue to this day.

In times of global crisis, immigrants have consistently taken the weight of America's tendency toward prejudice. During World War II, for instance, Japanese immigrants and their American-born children were put in internment camps after Pearl Harbor was attacked, and the government refused to take in Jewish refugees fleeing the Nazis for fear that some of them might be German spies. Today, as the United States struggles out of economic recession and as terror in the Middle East rises, it once again points fingers at immigrants; according to some, Latinx ruined the economy and Syrian refugees are all potential ISIS members. In a poll by Morning Consult, a nonpartisan media and technology company, about 53 percent of American voters believe Middle Eastern immigrants have a negative effect on American society, despite there being no evidence to support that belief, and about 38 percent believe the same about Latinx. These beliefs are most common among white voters.

## STAYING VIGILANT

"They may say, 'Well, it's under our constitutional purview to be able to do this and be able to register and keep an eye on all persons who are not citizens.' But it's what you do with that registry, what concerns me. And in World War II, when they gathered [Japanese Americans] up, they broke— the government broke the law again by using the census data, and the census data is supposed to be private. So, I think that we still have to be vigilant about what our government does."
—Representative Mike Honda, about why he opposes a registry of Muslims

Mike Honda, interview by Nermeen Shaikh and Amy Goodman, "Rep. Honda, Survivor of Japanese Internment Camp, Decries Trump Proposal for Muslim Registry," Democracy Now!, December 15, 2016. www.democracynow.org/2016/12/15/rep_honda_survivor_of_japanese_internment.

This is not to say that everyone who opposes immigration is racist, but the evidence suggests a racial bias in Americans— specifically in white Americans—against those of Latin American, Middle Eastern, and African origin. Whether or not people realize it, their culture shapes the way they think about themselves in relation to others, and America's mainly white, Christian-geared media gives the illusion that white, Christian people are the "norm." Therefore, when white Americans look out into the world, they see many people who do not look like them or believe the same things as them and deem them wrong. In the case of immigration, Americans worry that immigrants will challenge the country's values and make America worse in some way.

After Trump was elected president, the number of hate crimes against nonwhite people—citizens and noncitizens alike—rose dramatically. Muslim women have reported being screamed at for wearing a hijab (a religious headscarf) and having their hijabs pulled off by people calling them terrorists. Even children have experienced the negative impact of racism. In a survey of teachers by the Southern Poverty Law Center, a nonprofit social justice group, "more than two-thirds of the teachers ... reported that their students—mainly Muslims, immigrants and children of immigrants—were worried about what could happen to them and their families after the November election. And more than one-third of the teachers said they've noticed a rise in anti-immigrant and anti-Muslim sentiment among their students as well."[43] Although some Americans support such sentiments, others strongly believe this kind of reaction and behavior, in children and adults, is unacceptable, especially in a democracy.

*The repercussions of the 2016 election have made some children feel unsafe in their own classrooms.*

## Into the Future

With a Republican majority in the House and Senate as of 2017, Trump may be capable of having his campaign promises become reality, and after years of back and forth, America could see a significant shift in immigration policy. Many immigrants in America, however, fear that their future might be bleak. While some are safe from deportation, others could face losing their jobs and being separated from their families. However, major demonstrations and public displays of support for immigrants have shown that many Americans still want to work toward building a better future for everyone who lives in the country, regardless of where they come from. The immigration debate has been part of the national dialogue in America since its earliest days, and it continues to play a major part in American society and politics today.

## Introduction: The Great Immigration Debate

1. "Peaceful Protests End with Disturbance at March," CBS 2 News, Los Angeles, May 2, 2007.

2. Quoted in Daniel Gonzalez, "Marchers Re-Energized Amid Immigration Push," *Arizona Republic*, May 2, 2007.

## Chapter 1: A Nation of Immigrants

3. *Merriam-Webster Online*, s.v. "immigrant," accessed December 2, 2016. www.merriam-webster.com/dictionary/immigrant.

4. Herbert S. Klein, *A Population History of the United States*. New York, NY: Cambridge University Press, 2004, p. 83.

5. Francis Walker, "Restriction of Immigration," *Atlantic Monthly*, June 1896.

## Chapter 2: Immigration in the 21st Century

6. Sharon R. Ennis, Merarys Ríos-Vargas, and Nora G. Albert, "The Hispanic Population: 2010," U.S. Census Bureau, May 2011. www.census.gov/prod/cen2010/briefs/c2010br-04.pdf.

7. Diego Laje and Corinna Liu, "Why Asians Want to Move to the U.S.," CNN, July 19, 2012. www.cnn.com/2012/07/19/business/asia-u-s-immigrants.

8. "Immigration and Urban Sprawl," Federation for American Immigration Reform, October 2002. www.fairus.org/site/PageServer?pagename=iic_immigrationissuecentersb1cc.

9. Ted Hesson, "Why American Cities Are Fighting to Attract Immigrants," *The Atlantic*, July 21, 2015. www.theatlantic.com/business/archive/2015/07/us-cities-immigrants-economy/398987.

10. Quoted in Michael Martinez, "At 104 Degrees, the Forecast Is Death," *Chicago Tribune*, March 18, 2007.

11. Quoted in Martinez, "At 104 Degrees, the Forecast Is Death."

12. Walter Ewing, Ph.D., Daniel E. Martínez, Ph.D., and Rubén G. Rumbaut, Ph.D., "The Criminalization of Immigration in the United States," American Immigration Council, July 13, 2015. www.americanimmigrationcouncil.org/research/criminalization-immigration-united-states.

## Chapter 3: Immigration and the Economy

13. Daniel T. Griswold, "The Need for Comprehensive Immigration Reform: Serving Our National Economy," The Cato Institute, May 26, 2005.

14. Steven A. Camarota, "The High Cost of Cheap Labor," Center for Immigration Studies, August 2004. www.cis.org/articles/2004/fiscal.html.

15. Quoted in Nina Bernstein, "Tax Returns Rise for Immigrants in U.S. Illegally," *New York Times*, April 16, 2007.

16. Quoted in Bernstein, "Tax Returns Rise for Immigrants in U.S. Illegally."

17. Quoted in Nicole Akoukou Thompson, "How Are Marketers Reaching Latinos? Top Hispanic Marketers Discuss 2014's Marketing Strategies, What to Expect in 2015," *Latin Post*, December 29, 2014. www.latinpost.com/articles/29110/20141229/expert-marketing-opinions-3-top-hispanic-marketers-discuss-2014s-marketing-strategies-and-what-to-expect-in-2015.htm.

18. Maria E. Enchautegui, "Immigrant and Native Workers Compete for Different Low-Skilled Jobs," *The Urban Intitute*, October 14, 2015. www.urban.org/urban-wire/immigrant-and-native-workers-compete-different-low-skilled-jobs.

19. Quoted in Steven Greenhouse, "Low Pay and Broken Promises Greet Guest Workers," *New York Times*, February 28, 2007.

20. Quoted in Myung Oak Kim, Fernando Quintero, and Laura Frank, "Some Firms Play Loose with the Law," *Rocky Mountain News*, February 27, 2007.

21. "Border Patrol Overview," U.S. Customs and Border Protection, January 27, 2015. www.cbp.gov/border-security/along-us-borders/overview.

## Chapter 4: Adjusting to American Culture

22. Peter D. Salins, "The Assimilation Contract: Endangered but Still Holding," in *Reinventing the Melting Pot: The New Immigrants and What It Means to Be American*, ed. Tamar Jacoby. New York, NY: Basic Books, 2004, p. 102.

23. "Muslim Americans: Middle Class and Mostly Mainstream," Pew Research Center, May 22, 2007. www.pewresearch.org/2007/05/22/muslim-americans-middle-class-and-mostly-mainstream.

24. Samuel P. Huntington, *Who Are We? The Challenges to America's National Identity*. New York, NY: Simon & Schuster, 2004, p. 12.

25. Huntington, *Who Are We?*, p. 142.

26. Luis R. Fraga and Gary M. Segura, "Culture Clash? Contesting Notions of American Identity and the Effects of Latin American Immigration," *American Political Science Association Perspectives*, June 2006, p. 281.

27. Peter Skerry, "'This Was Our Riot, Too': The Political Assimilation of Today's Immigrants," in *Reinventing the Melting Pot*, p. 227.

28. Gregory Rodriguez, "Mexican Americans Are Building No Walls," *Los Angeles Times*, February 29, 2004.

29. Stephan Thernstrom, "Rediscovering the Melting Pot: Still Going Strong," in *Reinventing the Melting Pot*, p. 52.

30. Julia Preston, "Newest Immigrants Assimilating as Fast as Previous Ones, Report Says," *New York Times*, September 21, 2015. www.nytimes.com/2015/09/22/us/newest-immigrants-assimilating-as-well-as-past-ones-report-says.html.

31. Tara Bahrampour, "Study: Legal Mexican Immigrants Become U.S. Citizens at a Lower Rate Than Others," *Washington Post*, February 4, 2013. www.washingtonpost.com/local/study-legal-mexican-immigrants-become-us-citizens-at-a-lower-rate-than-others/2013/02/04/a3751d30-6f0a-11e2-ac36-3d8d9dcaa2e2_story.html?utm_term=.e06580ce3b86.

32. Jack Citrin, Amy Lerman, Michael Murakami, and Kathryn Pearson, "Testing Huntington: Is Hispanic Immigration a Threat to American Identity?," *American Political Science Association Perspectives on Politics*, March 2007, p. 35.

33. George J. Borjas, "Economic Assimilation: Trouble Ahead," in *Reinventing the Melting Pot*, p. 203.

## Chapter 5: The Future of Immigration

34. "Immigration Reform," Hillary for America, 2016. www.hillaryclinton.com/issues/immigration-reform.

35. "Who We Are," U.S. Immigration and Customs Enforcement. www.ice.gov/about.

36. Alejandra Marchevsky and Beth Baker, "Why Has President Obama Deported More Immigrants Than any President in US History?," *The Nation*, March 31, 2014. www.thenation.com/article/why-has-president-obama-deported-more-immigrants-any-president-us-history.

37. Quoted in Elliot Spagat, "Immigration Raids Net Many Not on the Radar," *Associated Press*, April 6, 2007.

38. H.B.C., "The Economist Explains: What Are Sanctuary Cities?," *The Economist*, November 22, 2016. www.economist.com/blogs/economist-explains/2016/11/economist-explains-13.

39. Quoted in H.B.C., "The Economist Explains."

40. "Testimony of Anne C. Richard, Assistant Secretary for the Bureau of Population, Refugees, and Migration to the House Judiciary Committee, Immigration and Border Security Subcommittee Hearing on 'The Syrian Refugee Crisis and Its Impact on the Security of the U.S. Refugee Admissions Program,'" House of Representatives Judiciary Committee, November 19, 2015. judiciary.house.gov/wp-content/uploads/2016/02/Richard-Statement-House-Judiciary-11-19-15.pdf.

41. Miriam Valverde, "Reince Priebus Says Trump, Congress Have Similar Immigration Policies," PolitiFact, November 18, 2016. www.politifact.com/truth-o-meter/statements/2016/nov/18/reince-priebus/reince-priebus-says-trump-congress-have-similar-im.

42. "Executive Order: Protecting the Nation from Foreign Terrorist Entry into the United States," the White House, January 27, 2017. www.whitehouse.gov/the-press-office/2017/01/27/executive-order-protecting-nation-foreign-terrorist-entry-united-states.

43. Christina Wilkie, "'The Trump Effect': Hatred, Fear and Bullying on the Rise in Schools," *Huffington Post*, April 13, 2016. www.huffingtonpost.com/entry/trump-effect-southern-poverty-law-center_us_570e8619e4b03d8b7b9f2836.

# DISCUSSION QUESTIONS

## Chapter 1: A Nation of Immigrants

1. What factors limited immigration to America between 1789 and 1814?

2. What was the first federal act to limit immigration, and why was it passed?

3. What direction did immigration in the United States take after Congress passed the Hart-Celler Act of 1965?

## Chapter 2: Immigration in the 21st Century

1. How is the modern image of the immigrant changing?

2. Why has Asian immigration increased over the last decade?

3. Why are immigrants often thought of as criminals?

## Chapter 3: Immigration and the Economy

1. Why do unauthorized immigrants pay taxes?

2. How important are remittances to the Mexican economy?

3. Why are immigration laws becoming more strictly enforced?

## Chapter 4: Adjusting to American Culture

1. How does Samuel Huntington's view of national identity differ from that of Luis R. Fraga and Gary M. Segura?

2. What benefits are there to becoming a U.S. citizen?

3. What are the advantages and disadvantages of bilingual education and English language immersion?

## Chapter 5: The Future of Immigration

1. What are the arguments for and against unauthorized immigrants remaining in the country? Which argument do you feel is the most compelling, and why?

2. Why have some cities become sanctuary cities?

3. Do you agree or disagree with the immigration policies that have been proposed by the Trump administration? Why?

## American Immigration Council
1331 G Street NW, Suite 200
Washington, D.C. 20005
(202) 507-7500
www.americanimmigrationcouncil.org
The American Immigration Council is a nonprofit, nonpartisan organization committed to sensible and humane immigration policies as well as challenging myths and misconceptions about immigrants.

## The Brookings Institution
1775 Massachusetts Avenue NW
Washington, D.C. 20036
(202) 797-6000
www.brookings.edu
The Brookings Institution is a private, nonprofit organization devoted to independent research and innovative policy solutions.

## Federation for American Immigration Reform (FAIR)
25 Massachusetts Avenue NW, Suite 330
Washington, D.C. 20001
(202) 328-7004
www.fairus.org
FAIR is a national, nonprofit, public-interest membership organization of concerned citizens who share a common belief that America's immigration policies must be reformed to serve the national interest.

**National Association of Counsel for Children (NACC)**
13123 E. 16th Avenue, B390
Aurora, CO 80045
(888) 828-NACC
www.naccchildlaw.org
This organization gives legal aid to children and families. Immigrant children who need legal help can contact the NACC for advice.

**Pew Research Center**
1615 L Street NW, Suite 800
Washington, D.C. 20036
(202) 419-4300
www.pewresearch.org
This nonpartisan organization provides information on the issues, attitudes, and trends shaping America and the world. It does so by conducting public opinion polling and social science research, reporting news and analyzing news coverage, and holding forums and briefings. It does not take positions on policy issues.

# FOR MORE INFORMATION

## Books

Coan, Peter Morton. *Ellis Island Interviews: In Their Own Words*. New York, NY: Checkmark Books, 1997.
This collection of interviews details the stories of just some of the many people who came to America through Ellis Island.

Gagne, Tammy. *Immigration in the U.S.* Hockessin, DE: Mitchell Lane Publishing, 2014.
The author provides a nonpartisan summary of immigration laws in the United States.

Howell, Sara. *Undocumented Immigrants*. New York, NY: PowerKids Press, 2015.
This book takes an in-depth look at what it means to be an undocumented immigrant, reasons for immigrating illegally, and struggles in American society for undocumented immigrants.

Klein, Herbert S. *A Population History of the United States*. New York, NY: Cambridge University Press, 2004.
This book gives a statistical history of population growth in the United States, with interesting facts about immigration and its effect on population.

Leavitt, Amie Jane. *U.S. Immigration Services*. Hockessin, DE: Mitchell Lane Publishing, 2014.
This is a guide for immigrants who are working on becoming citizens, including personal stories from immigrants going through the naturalization process and information about services available for immigrants.

Osborne, Linda Barrett. *This Land Is Our Land: A History of American Immigration*. New York, NY: Abrams Books for Young Readers, 2016.
The author gives a comprehensive history of government policy and popular response to immigrants in America between 1800 and 1965.


# Websites

### Center for Immigration Studies
www.cis.org
This comprehensive website features information, news articles, and opinions favoring immigration control and reform in the United States.

### It's My Life: Immigration
pbskids.org/itsmylife/family/immigration/index.html
This website includes stories from real immigrant kids and facts about immigration, as well as activities such as interactive polls and a word search.

### National Immigration Forum
www.immigrationforum.org
This website features details on legislation, articles, and opinions favoring less restriction in immigration.

### U.S. Census Bureau
www.census.gov
Find detailed statistical demographic information on the U.S. population dating back to the first census ever taken in 1790. Information about the foreign-born population and immigration history can also be found here.

### U.S. Customs and Border Protection
www.cbp.gov
This is the official website for the CBP, which handles the task of protecting America's borders. Learn about the CBP's job in great detail, as well as what life is like for a Border Patrol agent.

# INDEX

# PICTURE CREDITS

Cover Andy Cross/The Denver Post via Getty Images; p. 7 Ryan Rodrick Beiler/Shutterstock.com; p. 9 Spencer Platt/Getty Images; p. 14 johnbraid/Shutterstock.com; pp. 18 (left), 20 (top and bottom) courtesy of the Library of Congress; p. 18 (right) Universal History Archive/UIG via Getty Images; p. 23 LBJ Library photo by Yoichl Okamoto; p. 27 © istockphoto.com/rrodrickbeiler; p. 30 © istockphoto.com/szefei; p. 36 © istockphoto.com/vichinterlang; p. 37 © istockphoto.com/PatrickPoendl; pp. 38–39 Education Images/UIG via Getty Images; p. 45 John Moore/Getty Images; p. 48 Ariel Skelley/Blend Images/Getty Images; p. 51 evok20/iStock/Thinkstock; p. 53 © istockphoto.com/TerryJ; p. 56 Sherry V Smith/Shutterstock.com; p. 57 Robert Nickelsberg/Getty Images; p. 61 Jeremy Woodhouse/Blend Images/Thinkstock; p. 65 Cindy Ord/Getty Images for NYCWFF; p. 67 Polarpx/Shutterstock.com; p. 68 SAUL LOEB/AFP/Getty Images; p. 70 Joe Raedle/Getty Images; p. 72 Pressmaster/Shutterstock.com; p. 75 Visions of America/UIG via Getty Images; p. 76 MARK RALSTON/AFP/Getty Images; p. 78 Charles Reed/U.S. Immigration and Customs Enforcement via AP; p. 80 Scott Olson/Getty Images; pp. 82–83 Songquan Deng/Shutterstock.com; p. 85 thomas koch/Shutterstock.com; p. 90 © istockphoto.com/Tomwang112.

# ABOUT THE AUTHOR

**Michelle Denton** is a recent graduate of Canisius College. She holds a bachelor's degree in English and creative writing and graduated cum laude from the All-College Honors Program. She lives in Buffalo, New York, where she works as props master at the Subversive Theatre Collective, and she is in the process of having her first stage play produced there. This is her first title for Lucent Press.